The
Healthy Hens
Handbook

The
Healthy Hens
Handbook

Terry Beebe

The Goodlife Press

The Healthy Hens Handbook

Published in 2013 by The Good Life Press Ltd.,
PO Box 536, Preston, Lancashire, PR2 9ZY
www.homefarmer.co.uk

Text and photographs © 2013 Terry Beebe

ISBN 978-1-907866-08-1

A catalogue record for this book is available from the British Library.

We celebrate the fact that The Healthy Hens Handbook is printed in the United Kingdom by one of the few remaining colour book printers. With so much printing going overseas, we maintain it's just as important to support the UK's manufacturing industry alongside local food initiatives.

Thank you for buying this book.

Photo Credits
Cover photo and page 8 - © Hayden Wood istock, page 57 © Heiko Kiera - Fotolia.com,
page 58 © JavaJunkie - Fotolia.com, pages 64 and 65 Joanna Mudhar,
page 67 © Tom Bayer - Fotolia.com, page 92 and 93 - www.chickenvet.com, page 121 Ian Hazlehurst,
page 149 - www.poultrykeeper.com, page 160-161 - © Leca Isabelle - Fotolia.com,
page 201 - www.poultrykeeper.com, page 203 - R. Tott.

Printed in the UK by Bell & Bain Ltd., Glasgow.

Contents

Foreword

Having known Terry Beebe for a good many years, and seen the quality of the birds he's capable of breeding, it comes as no surprise to me that a publisher has finally taken the opportunity of tapping into his wealth of knowledge and experience by commissioning him to write this book. There can be few poultry enthusiasts currently out there who've achieved more than he, not only with his beloved Poland but, in a wider sense across the Fancy, too.

His efforts to bolster the Poland Club over the years have been admirable, as has been his determination to help those seeking his advice and guidance. He's been happy to share his expertise but, at the same time, has never shied away from telling people the truth about their birds, even when it's perhaps not been quite what they wanted to hear!

Terry is a great believer in breeding poultry properly. He's not one of those who likes to dabble with new colours, or cross this breed with that one in the hope of producing something to catch a passing craze. He's a breeder who understands the importance of sticking to the established standard, of helping conserve breeds that are heading towards trouble and of working sensibly with poultry to make a worthwhile difference.

Although he's kept and bred various forms of waterfowl and turkeys over the years, and enjoys a keen interest in Old English Game and birds of prey, his pragmatic approach to his chickens has always ensured that he's never spread himself too thinly. He's simply specialised in the few breeds that interest him most, and done an enviable job with them all. It's all too easy with chickens to be tempted down too many roads, so you end up over-committed with different breeds and never really develop a proper understanding of any of them as a result. To his credit, Terry's never fallen into this trap.

So it's these qualities of patient yet determined learning and expertise through experience, which I hope will shine out from the pages of this book. I know first hand, from the work that Terry's done for me in Practical Poultry over the years, that he has a burning desire to help newcomers to the hobby do things correctly. He feels strongly that beginners need the best possible guidance when it comes to the welfare of their hens, and he has all the attributes required to deliver it.

So, if just a fraction of Terry's enthusiasm for the subject leaps out at you from the pages of this book, then you'll be a better poultry keeper as a result. Never forget that your hens are entirely dependent upon you for their health and welfare; if you slip up, they're the ones that suffer. So take heed of the practical, down-to-earth advice given, and use it to help ensure that your birds live happy and productive lives while in your care.

Chris Graham, Editor,
Practical Poultry magazine

Introduction

Who is this Book Aimed at?

Keeping chickens is actually a great pastime and hobby, and one that is now being enjoyed by people all over the world, and increasingly so as each year passes. What has changed dramatically since the days of our grandparents is the fact that chickens were originally kept solely as a food source for the family, but now the hobby of poultry keeping has taken a different turn, with many new keepers keeping them as what can only be described as family pets. In this manner the birds very quickly become an integral part of your daily life with routines often geared to poultry keeping chores, and in truth there are very few pets that can claim to be both companions and at the same time productive. This is, however, true of chickens; they do make good pets, each with their individual characters, and no-one would disagree that they are useful producers of eggs.

This book is aimed at chicken keepers of all levels, from the starter with a couple of newly acquired laying birds to the more experienced keeper with a couple of dozen. As such it pays special attention to the day-to-day routine of basic management and maintenance required to keep your birds in good health and condition. You are their appointed keeper and it is your role to do this, both legally and morally, but it is a chore which, like most keepers, you will, for the most part at least, and barring severe rain, do voluntarily, cheerfully and even gratefully if your birds give you the same level of satisfaction mine have given me over the years.

Chickens are actually quite easy to keep and generally look after themselves as they would have done in the wild but, dependent on the time of year, they can become quite time consuming. The winter months are probably the most difficult time for a keeper, but provided you have a well organised daily routine that makes sure the birds are well looked after and covers all their basic needs such as safe shelter, clean water and food, the results will undeniably give you great pleasure as well as fresh eggs for your breakfast.

The welfare of your birds must always be uppermost in your mind as a chicken keeper and

A Silver Laced Poland bantam.

special attention has been paid throughout this book to cover all aspects of looking after and keeping chickens. It has been my aim to provide as much information as possible with regard to the *correct* methods of poultry keeping and breeding, using very basic and easy to understand advice. Keeping chickens is definitely not rocket science and as such is within the abilities of all of us. What does, however, often seem to be lacking in many of today's publications is the answers to many of the simple and very basic questions of husbandry that we are asked every day. When you are starting out there is no such thing as a trivial question and I have tried to include answers to them, together with the more complex and in-depth questions you will be asking a little later when moulting begins, or one of your hens goes broody.

Although the book is primarily intended as a health reference book for your birds I have concentrated on emphasizing management techniques and the typical chicken keeper's routine, as it is by doing this responsibly and well that you will best maintain the long term health of your birds. I have also covered all aspects of chicken keeping, from buying your first chicken, housing your birds, hatching your own chickens by incubation or natural rearing, general maintenance including day-to-day poultry management through to keeping a larger flock, whether for eggs, meat, exhibition, or simply for the pleasure of having them as pets. All these factors are equally important as the right bird for the right job will always perform best and with fewer problems, and they will thrive in good, dry housing conditions and clearly benefit from the very best possible start in life.

A Brief Word about the Author

Terry was born in Calow near Chesterfield in Derbyshire. For the first few years of his life the family lived with his grandparents and it was during these early years that his interest in chickens began.

His grandfather George Redvers Beebe was both a keen gardener and chicken keeper and his own preferred breed was Rhode Island Reds, with the birds keeping the family in both eggs and meat.

Then a few years later the school which Terry attended took on its own flock of chickens as part of the school's education programme, and it was Terry who became school chicken keeper.

After leaving school Terry's parents wanted him to have a secure job and he spent the next few years working in men's outfitting until he met and married Clare. Buying a house and living more in the countryside allowed him to rekindle his early interest in birds, and he kept several different breeds, becoming very well known for the Poland breed of chicken, an exhibition bird with a crested head and bred in several different colours. Over the years Terry and Clare produced many show winners, including Show Champion at shows such as the Royal Show, the Bakewell Show and many other major events. Both Clare and Terry also became Poultry Club judges and have for many years been very heavily involved in all aspects of poultry keeping.

Terry is a contributor to several well known UK poultry magazines and has his own magazine in the USA. He also appears on TV when questions of poultry welfare arise and does a monthly question and answers column in a major UK poultry magazine. He is therefore well aware of the concerns and questions often asked by poultry

A Bluebell.

keepers of all levels. With over 20 years of full-time experience with a large variety of different breeds and considerable time spent working alongside some of the top experts in the UK, USA and Europe, he has acquired a wide working knowledge and understanding, much of it now put to use helping to improve the knowledge of people new to the hobby of keeping chickens.

Terry now lives in Lincolnshire where he plays an active part in the local Poultry Club scene.

Blue Orpingtons.

A Brief History of Chickens

The chickens we see today are all descended from the Jungle Fowl, *Gallus domesticus*, and the original in its wildest form was known as the Red Jungle Fowl, *Gallus Gallus*. This bird still exists today in various parts of Asia, and because of this it is possible to compare them with today's domesticated birds. These direct descendants of those original fowl are certainly rather more agile and active than our own more docile domesticated breeds, and in most cases rather more aggressive too.

Research shows that birds were crossbred with the Grey Jungle Fowl, *G. Sonneratii*, to produce a yellow skin about 8000 years ago in what was probably the very first step in the development of the hybrid chickens with which we are all familiar today. This development has continued over the centuries, producing many different breeds, most of which were created as a source of food, supplying us with both meat and eggs – the luxury of chickens as pets was still a long way off at this point!

A degree of uncertainty surrounds the very earliest origins of the domesticated chicken with which we are all familiar today. They are thought to have arrived in Eastern Europe in about 3000BC and in Western Europe in about 1000BC. Until recently it was understood to have been first domesticated in China in around 6000BC, but there is an alternative view that today's birds originated in the Indus Valley in what is now Pakistan around 2500BC. The very earliest domesticated birds in Asia, Africa and Europe were probably used solely for fighting purposes.

Many civilizations involved the birds in aspects of their religious ceremonies; in Indonesia, for example, a chicken was used in a cremation ceremony, with the bird tethered by the leg for the duration of the service – it was believed that any evil spirits would enter the chicken and not the families present at the service. After the ceremony the chicken was simply taken back to carry on with its normal life.

In Ancient Greece chickens were regarded as an exotic species which usually exempted them from sacrifice; cocks in particular were said to have great valour which related to Gods such as Hercules, Athena and Ares. They also believed that lions were frightened of cocks, and I must admit that some of the more aggressive birds, especially during the breeding season, can be pretty intimidating, though perhaps not to a lion.

Chickens, and cocks (often called roosters) in particular, have been part of our everyday life for many centuries, with the tops of church steeples often adorned with them on weather vanes, possibly deriving from a belief that the large comb on birds was somehow representative of a lightning strike, although the main aim was really to indicate nothing more than wind direction.

Throughout the world the evolution of the chicken still continues year-by-year, even today, with new specialist breeds with ever more specific purposes being devised and created, and with hybrids and traditional breeds often living together in flocks. There has been an unprecedented increase in interest in keeping poultry, some of it perhaps due to the rehousing of former battery hens by the British Hen Welfare Trust, but this increase in interest has undoubtedly helped to save many of our heritage rare breeds too, as people's interests in poultry have developed from perhaps a couple of ex-battery birds to more specialized keeping. This has resulted in the development of new types of poultry keeper, with many pure breeds of both chickens and waterfowl today kept solely for exhibition purposes or as pets. There are, however, still many breeders who keep and breed pure breed production flocks for commercial use, which helps to keep alive original blood lines for future generations.

Black Rock.

ISA Brown commercial hens

Chapter One

Chicken Keeping and the Law

With the changes in poultry keeping over the years, the hybrid chicken has become a very popular choice of bird to keep. The production of these hybrid birds is invariably the result of some very intensive cross breeding using the genes and attributes of existing pure breeds, and this has enabled breeders to produce birds that are very desirable for their excellent high production abilities, specifically egg laying.

It is not illegal to keep chickens, whether in the back garden, on an allotment or free range in the countryside, unless the local authorities and, in some cases, the house builders, have introduced any rules or regulations to the contrary. A number of areas, including some new housing and estates, both in towns and in the country too, are now covered by restrictions relating to the keeping of livestock of any kind. Be sure to check either before moving, and certainly before buying any poultry. When you do buy a property, any rules regarding the keeping of livestock or any other restrictions will be written into the deeds, with some stating specifically that it is not allowed, although there are currently numerous ongoing challenges under an earlier statute which gave people an apparent automatic right to keep chickens, but not all livestock. At present there are no nationwide restrictions in place on the keeping of birds, merely a number of more regional and local covenants that might prove an obstacle, many probably introduced as a reaction to the increasing popularity of garden birds. Before deciding to keep chickens, consult with your local council to check whether there have been any by-laws passed with regard to the keeping of poultry in your area. Councils will try to enforce these, so it could save you both the considerable inconvenience of a prosecution and the grief of having to give up your birds at a later date.

One clear rule is that, at the time of writing, if you keep more than fifty birds you are legally bound to register them for the purposes of disease management should an outbreak or epidemic occur in your region. To do this you must notify Defra for their GB Poultry Register which was set up in 2005.

There are certain simple tips which should help

Welsummer cockerel.

to prevent any problems with regard to keeping chickens:

Check just how close the neighbours are, and in most cases avoid keeping cocks as their 'crowing' can cause considerable problems over noise levels with neighbours. If you live in an area where the noise might cause problems, try to buy birds that are already sexed as this will ensure that you have only hens.

Make sure that your birds are secure and not able to do any damage to other people's properties.

> *Chickens can cause serious damage to a garden and plants that may not be acceptable to a neighbour who happens to be a keen gardener. Seal off your own too using chicken wire!*

If you plan on keeping quite a few birds, consider what you will do to dispose of any chicken waste, including bedding; some can certainly be composted, but if there is an excessive amount arrangements will probably have to be made for its disposal. Any remaining waste could cause environmental problems with regard to both smell and possibly rodents, both of which should ideally be avoided. Chicken bedding and manure are both very good for composting, but the manure is full of nitrogen, which makes it far too strong to put directly onto your plants and flowers. However, once composted it makes an excellent fertiliser.

Also, be aware that anyone who is found to have been cruel to an animal of any kind, or has fallen short in providing for its welfare needs, may be banned from owning animals, fined up to £20,000

A Silkie cross known as a Goldie.

Silkie cross-bred layers.

and/or sent to prison. If you do decide to keep chickens, or any other livestock, for that matter, there are no exemptions – you are responsible for them, and this legislation has been designed to make sure that you fulfil that role. Fortunately, it is not difficult to implement and, in the light of how we view animals in the twenty first century, it is actually very reasonable. Like all legislation, however, it is likely to change at some point in the future, so keep an eye on the Defra website at www.gov.uk/defra for an up-to-date summary of your obligations and any likely future amendments to them.

When you do eventually become a chicken keeper you will be bound by the Animal Welfare Act 2006 which makes owners and keepers responsible for ensuring that the welfare needs of their animals are met. These include the need:

for a suitable environment (place to live).

for a suitable diet.

to exhibit normal behaviour patterns.

to be housed with, or apart from, other animals (if applicable).

to be protected from pain, injury, suffering and disease.

Barnevelder

Chapter Two

The Chicken – Inside and Out

As a chicken keeper it is a good idea to have at least some knowledge of the basic structure of a chicken. This information will help you to understand some of the changes and occasional problems which may take place throughout the year.

Chickens are warm-blooded creatures that develop for the most part outside the mother's body. The birds are very quick to mature and are virtually self-sufficient within just a couple of days of hatching. Although warmth is needed in the early stages, birds feather up very quickly and can normally forage outside for themselves after about five or six weeks, and sometimes even less, depending on the weather conditions.

All chickens have a largely cream or white coloured skin, with the exception of the Silkie, which has a dark blue/grey skin.

The Digestive System

Adult chickens have no teeth, hence the saying 'as rare as hens' teeth'. They instead have a digestive system that allows them to break down their food. A bird first pecks and picks up the food, which is then swallowed whole. This passes into the gullet and then on into the crop, which acts as a storage area. Once the feed is in the crop it is moistened ready for it to be passed downwards into the 'proventriculus', also known as the 'true stomach'. From there it progresses into the gizzard, a sort of grinding machine with grit stored there to help the bird to 'grind up' the feed internally, which is then passed into the small intestine and on for digestion.

The Vent (Cloaca)

The word 'cloaca' effectively means 'sewer'. This is the end of the bird from which the egg emerges, and also the faeces. A female bird is actually able to turn part of her oviduct inside out while laying an egg, and this means that the egg comes out of the vent with no actual direct contact with the faeces. Birds cannot urinate and any items not absorbed into the blood pass into the large intestine from which they are passed out by the bird through the vent.

Brown Leghorn cockerel.

Black Silkie.

Respiratory/Breathing

All poultry will at some stage suffer from some type of respiratory problem. Birds have small lungs and these are interconnected through a series of air sacs. Birds cannot sweat, so to keep cool they 'pant', and by panting through the respiratory tract they are able to lose heat.

The Comb

This is the part of the chicken that in most cases sits on top of the head; they appear on both sexes, with males usually carrying a larger version. Combs are almost always red, but there are exceptions, these usually being purple.

> *The comb does have its uses and is not just there to make a bird look more attractive for mating. One of these uses is to help a bird control its temperature.*

The colour of the comb can also show when a bird is ready to mate. The comb will become a brighter red, showing a male bird that the hen in question is now ready, and at the same time showing other females that she is high in the pecking order.

Wattles

These are also used for temperature control and come in a great variety of sizes, depending on the breed; the males usually carry larger and more prominent wattles.

The Beak

The beak is a rather sensitive part of a chicken,

ISA Browns.

and, with no teeth as such, it is the beak which serves to 'cut' food such as leaves. This is made possible by the beak having a serrated edge.

The Wings

All chickens have wings, but most breeds certainly cannot fly any distance. They are mainly used to help them reach a roosting perch or for escape from danger, should the need arise. Clipping a single wing will greatly reduce a bird's confidence in its ability to fly by adversely affecting its sense of balance at the point of take-off. In most cases this is just enough to prevent it escaping over a wall or bush (and into a neighbour's garden!). The feathers will eventually grow back and, if done correctly, there is no adverse effect or pain caused to the bird.

A rescued ex-battery hen with feather loss.

White Star

Chapter Three

Know Your Chickens

You will need to research the various breed types before making your selection, as many breeds do have traits that may or may not be suitable for the environment in which you plan to keep the birds, or for the uses you may have in mind, such as egg or meat production. Visit as many suppliers as possible, and go to your local shows to see birds and to talk to breeders. This way you will be well prepared.

Domestic poultry is, for the most part, reasonably calm. Most chicken breeds are also not capable of long flights, but there are of course exceptions, especially when it comes to certain lighter breeds and a number of the game fowl breeds. If such birds are going to be your birds of choice then you will need to keep them in a suitable and appropriate environment.

It is always a good idea to take into account all aspects of your surroundings when selecting a breed; if you have acres of land and can let them free range, then larger breeds should not be a problem. If, however, space is very limited, careful consideration of the most suitable breeds will be necessary by taking into account both size and type.

You should also ask yourself exactly what you want from your birds; for example, do you want them to lay dark brown eggs, would a suitable meat producing bird be more appropriate, or do you just want some unusual and attractive birds for the garden, in which case the production side is probably not that important. If your choice of breed is dependent on them being able to supply good quality eggs then you will be best off with commercial hybrids which have usually been bred solely for the purpose of egg production. Such birds can usually be either confined or free range, subject to your choice and circumstances.

You could also consider some of the more exotic breeds that are a little bit different and often more attractive. There are also a number of good egg producing pure breeds which might be ideal, as they will provide variety in colour and appearance plus, depending on the breed you have chosen, a variation in egg shell colours, which could make your egg boxes look particularly spectacular.

All chickens today are divided into individual classes: the Pure Breeds (Soft Feather: Heavy, Soft Feather: Light, Hard Feather, True Bantam and Dual Purpose Breeds, with further breakdowns into a 'rare' category) and the modern range of Commercial Hybrids.

A selection of hybrids: left to right, White Star, Bluebells and a Speckledy.

When selecting a breed, the variation and number to choose from can be quite confusing, and even mind-blowing, especially for a beginner. You will need to decide just what you require from your birds, and this will narrow down the choice considerably, but they will need to fit your criteria if they are to function smoothly within a healthy flock. If you want your birds to breed and raise their own chicks you will need a breed that will sit and brood its own eggs, and hopefully prove to be good mothers who will rear their brood successfully. If they are to be solely for meat then look for a breed with some commercial meat value, both from the past and the present; there are broilers readily available that can be reared to a very good body size in a very short time. If you just want eggs then a typical ex-battery ISA Brown, the most common of today's commercial hybrids, will fit the bill.

If, on the other hand, your birds are to be kept solely for exhibition purposes then the main considerations will be type, quality and breed standard as stated by the Poultry Club. Most pure breed exhibition birds are *not* good layers due to the close breeding techniques used to achieve the required standard of perfection. They are usually also the most expensive to purchase, and often the very hardest to breed to the absolute correct standard required.

The Pure Breeds

Pure breeds are birds bred from within the same breed which enables the blood lines to be kept as pure as possible. Some 'out-crosses' may occur occasionally to improve a breed's standard, vigour and appearance, but the main aim is to keep the birds *as close to the original as possible*. The following classifications have been determined by the Poultry Club of Great Britain, which looks after the register of breeds in the UK. Bantam varieties are also available for most of these breeds.

The Soft Feather: Heavy breeds were originally developed as table birds and include the following breeds (opposite page):

Soft Feather: Heavy
Australorp
Barnevelder
Brahma
Cochin
Croad Langshan
Dorking
Faverolles
French Maran
Frizzle
German Langshan
Lincolnshire Buff
Maran
New Hampshire Red
Plymouth Rock
Rhode Island Red
Sussex
Wyandotte

Maran cock.

Australorp .

Frizzle.

Welsummer pullets.

Legbar.

The Soft Feather: Light breeds were developed primarily for their egg-laying abilities and include the following breeds:

Soft Feather: Light
Ancona
Andalusian
Araucana
Brabanter
Breda
Campine
Derbyshire Redcap
Friesian
Hamburg
Lakenvelder
Legbar
Leghorn
Minorca
Poland
Redcap
Rumpless Araucana
Scots Dumpy
Scots Grey
Silkie
Sultan
Sumatra
Vorwerk
Welbar
Welsummer
Yokahama

Dutch bantam hens.

Millefleur Japanese hen.

Both Light and Heavy breed classifications are based on weight and size, although the birds also have to be up to the specific standards of the classification required by the Poultry Club Standards of Exhibition. Most of the birds under this classification are soft feather breeds and include many well known and popular breeds we would all know and recognise.

Bantams

Bantams are a smaller version of any breed that has an equivalent in one of the larger varieties. Most large soft feather birds *do* have a bantam equivalent included in the standard.

True bantams are chickens that are *only* available in bantam form. They have no larger version of the breed, and many of them are very small indeed and suitable only for exhibition. Their size is also reflected in the very small eggs they produce.

True Bantams
Belgium
Booted
Dutch
Japanese
Modern Game
Nankin
Ohiki
Pekin
Rosecomb
Sebright
Serama

Old English Game.

Hard Feather Breeds

These were principally bred as fighting birds in times gone by. Today they include the game birds which are now bred for the far more pleasant pursuit of showing.

Hard Feather
Indian Game
Modern Game Bantam
Modern Game Large
Carlisle Old English Game
Old English Game Bantam
Oxford Old English Game

Asian Hard Feather
Asil
Ko Shamo
Kulang
Malay
Nankin Shamo
Satsumadori
Shamo
Taiwan
Thai Game
Tuzo
Yakido
Yamato-Gunkei

Norfolk Grey.

Rare Soft Feather Heavy
Cre'vecoeur
Dominique
German Langshan
Houdan
Ixworth
Jersey Giant
La Fl'eche
Modern Langshan
Norfolk Grey
North Holland Blue
Orloff
Rhodebar, Wybar.
Transylvanian Naked Neck

Rare Feather Light
Andalusian
Appenzeller
Marsh Daisy

Bantam Russian Orloff.

Brahma

Dual-purpose Breeds

Dual-purpose is a description covering breeds that are suitable for the production of both eggs and meat. Many of these are pure breed birds, and although blood lines are often now in decline, some are still available. All of today's hybrid chickens originated from pure breed dual-purpose birds, and the creation of these hybrids has taken many years to perfect in order to make sure they give the best possible combined production.

Dual-purpose Breeds
Barnevelder
Brahma
Dorking
Ixworth
Orpington
Plymouth Rock
Wyandotte

Black Orpington.

Hybrids

Hybrids are birds that are cross-bred using pure breeds to create new breeds that are usually suitable for high yield egg production. They are very popular, especially with the backyard keeper as a reliable egg producer.

There is no official recognition of these birds by the Poultry Club of Great Britain, and consequently there are no official opportunities to show these birds, although a number of smaller events do run a broader category in which *any* bird can be shown. Hybrid birds are usually produced solely to provide very good layers for commercial egg producers, and as such they make ideal back garden birds.

Breeding from hybrids, however, will be at best unpredictable. They are, for the most part, good-natured and become tame very quickly when in regular contact with people, making them excellent pets. The most familiar hybrids are the ISA Brown (the most likely ex-battery breed, and most common hybrid), the Black Rock/Barred Rock, the White Star, the Amber Star, the Bluebell, the Sussex, the Columbine and the Speckledy.

All of these breeds are readily available and inexpensive to purchase.

The bedrock of the commecial egg industry, hybrids are great layers.

Best Birds for Eggs

For anyone who only requires egg producing chickens it may be best to look at some of today's many commercial birds. These are usually cross breed commercials bred solely for egg production. The ISA Brown is probably the single best egg producer available today, but below are some good pure breed layers.

Egg-producing Breeds
Australorp
Dorking
Leghorn
Light Sussex
Rhode Island Red
Welsummer

ISA Brown. Probably the best egg producer.

Welsummer. An example of a good layer, but not a good sitter.

Leghorn. Another example of a good layer, but not a good sitter.

Hamburg.

Sitters and Non-sitters

Non-sitters are simply birds that will in most cases *not* raise their own chicks. It is the general rule that most light breeds belong to this classification. Consequently non-sitters are always least likely to become broody.

Sitters, on the other hand, are birds that *will* sit and rear their own chicks, most of these coming under the category of heavy breeds.

Some breeds such as Slikies are actually prone to broodiness, making them excellent sitters of acquired eggs. Most hybrids, on the other hand, have had broodiness virtually bred out of them, although there are exceptions as regards individual birds.

Non-Sitters
Ancona
Andalusian
Bresse
Campine
Hamburgh
Lakenvelder
Leghorn
Minorca
Old English Pheasant Fowl
Poland
Redcap
Scots Grey
Sicilian Buttercup
Spanish
Welsummer

The Healthy Hens Handbook

Seven Checks when Buying Poultry

Use the following basic checklist when buying your birds. Following these simple rules will help you to buy healthy birds in prime condition.

Look down the bird's throat, checking for any signs of sores or discharge as this could be an early sign of infection. Avoid birds showing any of these signs.

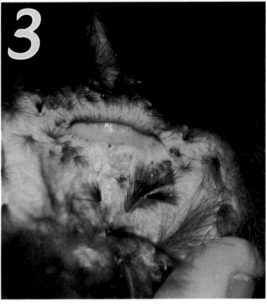

Check the breast bone by running your hand up it. Avoid any birds showing signs of a prominent and sharp breast bone as birds in this condition are unlikely to produce enough eggs to pay for their keep.

Check the vent area. It should be clean, dry and showing no signs of discharge or staining. A clean and dry vent is a sign of good health.

Size is important. Check the birds to make sure they are solid and reasonably heavy – a good weight is essential. A large abdomen is also nearly always an indication of a likely good layer.

A bird's stance is very important. Make sure they are standing upright with the tail held high. They should also look both strong and alert.

Check the plumage as feathers are an important indicator of a bird's well-being. They should be tight and close to the body. Fluffy or loose feathers are signs of unhealthy birds.

Small combs and wattles can be a sign of poor layers. Larger combs with a good red colour are usually signs of likely good layers.

Chapter Four

The Healthy Environment

Housing

Correct housing is perhaps the single most important issue when keeping chickens; whatever type of housing you choose it *must* provide a suitable and healthy environment for your birds. Consideration *must* be given to the type of breed being housed, and allowance made for their size and the number being housed. Always opt for a larger house than you actually need as this will enable you to add to the flock without overcrowding them. They will also be much happier and healthy this way.

> *There are actually no hard and fast rules that give preference to which type of housing you should use.*

There is a commonsense way to choose which will be the most suitable housing for both for the keeper *and* the birds. Essentially every poultry house needs to be water-proof, and rat- and fox-proof too, but still needs to have adequate ventilation without draughts. Take into account what you need by considering the following points:

Point One

The first consideration should be the essential day-to-day maintenance and cleaning required – how easy will it be to do this?

General everyday care should be straight forward and easy, and you need easy access to *all* parts of the housing. Can you physically get inside? If not is there easy access to all the nooks and crannies for cleaning? Many houses, especially arks, do not allow you to get inside – these will need to provide easy access through removable panels and doors that will allow you to clean easily from the outside, and to collect eggs from nest boxes.

A traditional wooden coop with wheels to make it easier to move around.

Point Two

Are the internal fittings easy to remove for cleaning?

Will the house be hard to deal with if you experience an insect infestation?

All types and sizes of poultry housing should ideally have removable fittings to enable you to maintain control over the internal conditions and inevitable insect problems – being able to remove perches, droppings boards and nest boxes makes keeping the internal environment clean and healthy a much easier task.

Point Three

Although it may look pretty, will you be able to work with the housing?

Too many fancy additions to a structure can only make life more difficult. Many houses have been produced to look very attractive in the back garden, and they do generally achieve this, but in some cases the housing may have areas that cannot be accessed easily as a result of the ornate design. Fancy design is of little use to a chicken, and could make your life far more difficult.

Housing which looks pretty in the garden is more of a priority for the keeper, but not for the birds. Many are actually not user-friendly when it comes to cleaning out or collecting eggs.

Point Four

Is the build quality strong and stable and able to withstand potential predator attacks?

When choosing, check the thickness of the timber for strength – the stronger the housing, the better, but also take into account the weight of the housing; will it need to be moved regularly to perhaps keep the ground fresh in an attached run? Examine the standard of the fittings too – these will need to be strong and of good quality. If a run is attached, the wire enclosing it will need to be a strong, good quality weld mesh – making sure that all of these items come up to standard will ensure that your birds are kept safe and protected. The cheapest option will most likely not prove to be the most economical one over time.

Point Five

Is the housing large enough for your birds?

What will be a suitable size for my chickens?

Housing sizes for chickens will depend on the breed and size of birds, and the number being kept – obviously smaller bantam breeds need a lot less space than the larger pure and commercial breeds, but whatever type of housing you choose there needs to be enough space to avoid overcrowding as this can lead to serious problems for the birds, such as feather pecking, and potentially cannibalism in extreme circumstances, or a greater likelihood of infestation. There are different recommended sizes, but as long as the birds are not overcrowded and given space there should be no problems. As a basic guideline for perching space, allow approximately 20cm (8in) per small bird and 30cm (12in) per large bird. Under *no* circumstances should you ever provide less than at least 1 metre to accommodate 5 larger fowl as this would constitute definite overcrowding. These figures are only a rough basic guide to give some idea as to what the recommendations are for housing numbers.

A Winscombe coop from Brinsea.

Make sure the housing has provision for plenty of fresh air.

Point Six

Is there good ventilation inside the housing?

Stale air can cause a variety of health problems, so make sure the housing has provision for plenty of fresh air, but without draughts. Ventilation is best provided by opening windows, especially in warm summer weather, or air vents in the coop such as ventilation holes covered with galvanized wire mesh. Ideally these vents should be able to open and close as required. Basic smaller houses usually have a number of small holes made in each end of the house which help ventilation. Do not be tempted to cover these up in winter.

Hygiene – the Cleaning Routine

General management and cleanliness of the housing is absolutely critical for the welfare of your birds. If you cannot provide the time each week to keep on top of it you may be subjecting your birds to a less than satisfactory environment.

> *Keeping your chickens in a clean and well managed environment will affect just how healthy they remain.*

In addition to regular daily and weekly regimes, there is also a need for all poultry keepers to carry out a full yearly check, together with a general overhaul for the different requirements of each season of the year. This needs to include repairs and a thorough cleaning out of the poultry housing, both inside and outside, plus all the equipment.

Often during the year there never seems quite enough time to carry out basic structural maintenance, so take time each new season to tackle all the jobs you may have planned to do, and

A Thornton poultry house.

get them done satisfactorily. These checks and overhauls also provide the perfect opportunity to give your birds a full checkout too.

The Need for Cleaning

I think that 'the need for cleaning' is in itself pretty obvious, but I do believe that the *reason* for requiring constant cleanliness should perhaps be explained. The single most important reason is the constant need to control disease; this has to be of the utmost importance for any chicken keeper, and being able to remove *all* internal items from the poultry housing to allow a full and thorough cleaning enables you to have as much control as possible over any potential spread of infection, disease and infestation through the flock. Housing that is allowed to become stale and infested is definitely no good for the poultry keeper and, more importantly, a serious threat to the birds' welfare. Droppings and fungus which can build up during long, damp winter nights in the coop with

rising temperatures are an ideal breeding ground for a wide range of common parasites.

A full clean and overhaul of the housing will not only remove bugs, dampness and the rather unpleasant ammonia smell which often hangs over a stale coop, especially during the winter months. Another consideration at all times, but especially as the weather warms up in spring and summer, is red mite, and cleaning is when you really need to try to control this pest before it takes control and causes you some very serious problems.

The whole of the area from the ceiling of the poultry unit to the ground on which it stands, plus any enclosed area in which the birds run, should all be checked. If the house and run can be moved to fresh, new ground this will give the present run area a chance to refresh and the grass time to grow back, but if moving the housing is not possible then a good and thorough cleanout of the run will be a good idea. Digging or rotavating the area will

Isa Browns

give the ground a new lease of life and freshen up the whole environment.

What you will achieve by carrying out this cleaning program is a suitable and safe environment for both yourself, and more importantly the birds, and with today's requirements regarding welfare, this care always has to be your main priority – there are no excuses for neglect; if you do not have the time to carry out the routine management of your birds then you need to consider whether or not you should be keeping them in the first place. I realise that this is blunt, but it is true.

Perches

Perches for poultry are just about as basic as you can get, but they are something which needs to be considered with care as they are very important for the long term health and wellbeing of your birds. The width of perches needs to be appropriate to accommodate the claws of the breed or breeds you keep, and if you use square new timber, always round off the edges to prevent damage to birds' feet. Try not to position perches too high as birds jumping down from too high a perch can cause problems such as bumblefoot. This is normally caused by a foreign object (sharp shavings or straw) penetrating the foot and turning septic, and landing from height is often a cause of the condition. Bumblefoot is normally visible as a swelling under the foot pad with a black spot in the centre. It can be hard to cure once the infection has occurred. It is not fatal but is very uncomfortable for an infected bird.

Perches should always be removable. This is to make cleaning easier, and especially to keep control of red mite which tend to group around the ends of perches and spend most of the daylight hours concealed in the nooks and crannies in which the perches rest. Use a good disinfectant, but if perches are too badly soiled, burn and replace them. I have used tree branches in the past, which actually work well but can be awkward to fit and keep clean. The use of branches is certainly an option if they are replaced on a regular basis –

Nest boxes and perches.

their natural roundness will probably be very comfortable for a bird's claws too.

There is a real need for perches for the birds to sleep on at night as this permits air to circulate both above and below, and keeps them clear of bedding and any droppings below. The width of each perch should be 4-5cm (1½-2in), with the edges slightly rounded to make it easier for the birds to grasp them whilst simultaneously removing any sharp edges that could damage a bird's feet. The length of a perch (or perches) should be 20cm (8in) of space per smaller bird, or 30cm (12in) per bird if the birds are large.

Always set perches higher than nest boxes to discourage the chickens from sleeping in the nest boxes. If there is more than one perch they will also need to be arranged so that one is not directly below another (for obvious reasons!), and with sufficient space in between to allow for comfortable roosting.

Always check the perches whilst cleaning them for

Maran and Legbar in next boxes.

any splits, damage or rough areas that might harm a bird's feet whilst it is roosting. If any damage is found, sand it down until smooth or replace it if the damage is considerable.

The Pop-hole

The 'pop-hole' is the entrance that allows the birds in and out of the house. Normally these are a sliding type shutter or a 'drop-down' ramp. Ideally the pop-hole will need to be accessible from outside the run (if you have one), giving you the option of not actually having to go *into* the run each time you let the birds out and shut them in safely for the night.

> *At night the pop-holes and any doors and windows should fasten firmly to exclude predators but permit ventilation.*

In addition to keeping out predators, door locks can also be useful in the effort to deter the increasing problem of thieves as poultry keeping becomes ever more popular. Pop-hole sizes need to be around 25cm (10in) wide x 30cm (12in) in height for standard breeds, but larger birds may need something slightly bigger at around 30 x 38cm (12 x 15in).

The Droppings Board

The idea here is that the droppings board will catch all or at least most of the droppings from the birds, especially during the night, and they can then be easily removed by sliding out the board for cleaning. An alternative such as thick plastic sheeting can be placed below the perches as this will work on the same principal, but it may be more difficult to remove. If your birds are housed in larger buildings such as sheds or outbuildings, a droppings pit or a box with a mesh cover or slats can be used and then cleaned out as required.

Nest Boxes

Every chicken house has, or at least should have, a

nest box or nesting area suitable for the birds to lay their eggs and brood chicks. Nest boxes come in many guises, from plain cardboard boxes, plastic fruit trays, buckets and home-made wooden boxes, to the very latest modern state of the art plastic and metal roll away designs.

The object of a nest box is simply to allow birds to feel safe and comfortable when laying their eggs, and to permit easy collection of the eggs by the keeper. For those of us who want our hens to hatch and rear their own chicks, the nest box also needs to offer a safe and secure refuge. When it comes to hatching and rearing chicks, however, there may need to be further changes to make them suitable for the purpose.

Question:

How many nest boxes will I need for the number of hens I keep?

Answer:

There are several answers as to how many nest boxes might be required for a given number of birds, and they always vary considerably, depending on who is giving the advice. The most popular recommendation is that there should be a nest box for every 4 to 5 birds, but it's really a matter of choice and space, and birds will usually use whichever nest box they prefer. It is in fact highly likely that your birds will use less than half the boxes you supply, with most off the eggs being laid in just a couple of boxes. It is even common for birds to *all* lay in the same nest box and ignore the remaining ones. Once you have installed nest boxes it will only take a few days to discover which and how many of them are actually used by the birds. It will probably become clear that nest boxes situated in darker areas within the shed are the most likely favourites.

Smaller flat pack poultry houses usually come with a nesting section, so in this type of housing the birds have little choice in the matter of where they lay.

Removable droppings boards make for easy cleaning.

A fun but practical coop by Green Frog Designs.

Plastic coops are a practical alternative for the back garden chicken keeper.
This range is manufactured by BEC Osprey.

Question:

What is the best type of bedding to use in nest boxes?

Answer:

There is a tendency to use straw or hay, but although this is what is often considered suitable for the birds and looks most comfortable, it is usually quite unsuitable, especially for the inside of a coop. If left undisturbed, straw will sweat unnoticed below the surface, creating deposits of mildew. This is one of the main causes of respiratory disease in chickens, and it also provides a perfect environment for insects and mite to live and breed as it is impossible to detect them beneath the surface. Leaving either straw or hay bedding unattended can eventually create severe health risks for birds, especially during warm weather or long winter nights when birds confined together for long periods can create a very warm and damp environment.

If you really feel a need to use straw, replace it *very* frequently, and use a powder such as Diatom regularly in the housing. As the box will inevitably become damp due to the straw sweating, use a product that will both dry and sanatise the environment. BioDri is ideal for this as it does both at the same time, keeping the boxes in a good, healthy condition and free from odours.

The ideal bedding is dust-extracted shavings. Put down a thick layer to fill the base of nest boxes to a reasonable depth and mix some good insect powder into the shavings to help keep the bedding parasite-free. To retain the shavings inside the nest box, make sure the front has a deep enough lip to prevent a rapid overspill. Ideally a depth of 3 or 4 inches of shavings will provide a soft base that will keep the birds in comfort while laying and help to prevent any eggs from being damaged.

Dust-extracted shavings are the ideal bedding solution.

> *Make sure the nest box is never left with a hard solid floor as this can cause egg breakages, which can lead to egg eating and a hygiene problem.*

Question:

What is the best way to clean out a nest box?

Answer:

Nesting areas should be easily accessible and nest boxes should be removable so that you can clean them *outside* the house. This will enable you to give them a really thorough clean and treat them for any other problems such as insect infestations.

A power washer is ideal, or use a really good disinfectant, leave them to dry then soak them again in something like Poultry Shield to protect and remove any traces of red mite. Keep removing boxes in regular use to check for any problems, and keep giving them a thorough clean, always replacing the bedding, and don't forget to add more insect powder for good measure.

If you have more than one wooden nest box it is a good idea to remove just one at a time to soak each one thoroughly, then allow it to dry completely before replacing it and doing the next one. If, however, you are using modern plastic type boxes it makes life a little easier as they are not porous and can be replaced back into the housing almost immediately after a good wipe down.

These new style nest boxes are also often fitted with a separate base that allows the eggs to roll forward and into a 'catch box' at the front, which prevents them from being damaged. In most cases no bedding needs to be added when they are in use, although you may choose to provide it to offer the birds greater comfort.

To use this type of box as a broody box you may have to adapt it by removing the egg tray base to make it more suitable for a broody hen.

Question:

Which parasites and insects are the worst threats to birds in the nest box?

Answer:

The nest box is inevitably an absolute haven for insects – it is, for the most part, reasonably undisturbed and is also warm and dark; an ideal environment in other words for insects to breed and remain undetected.

Lice are a common problem, but can be kept under control by keeping the boxes clean and powdered and changing the bedding regularly. They should be reasonably easy to keep under control, but the real cause for concern has to be red mite. They thrive in such environments, so a regular check at least every two or three days needs to be made to ensure they do not become established.

Nest Box Curtains

Egg laying hens love privacy, and this is why nest boxes situated in the darker areas inside the coop will be preferred. Site your nest boxes where there is least light, if you are able to. If your housing is very bright inside then you could use some type of covering draped over the front to darken the inside of the box, and by keeping the levels of light down to a minimum it will encourage the hens to lay. Sacking cloth or an old towel are ideal for this purpose and can be fastened to the top of the nest box and left hanging loosely over the entrance, but leave a small gap to one side to allow the birds easy access to the box.

Using this method works very well and costs very little, but it makes the hens more comfortable, increases egg production and helps to prevent any egg eating by the birds. When birds are laying in boxes with low levels of light, they are unable to see any previously laid eggs, and this helps to remove the temptation to peck away or eat any broken ones, as broken eggs in the coop are the single main cause of egg eating, and once this starts it can be extremely difficult to make them stop.

Mites will cause birds to stop laying, or make them lay their eggs in other places. The discomfort they cause can result in birds moving out and refusing

Laying hens love their privacy.

to return. This can become a serious issue if you are trying to collect the eggs and do not know where they are being laid, and for some chicken keepers a loss of eggs means a loss of profit.

The other very serious risk is for the health of a broody hen which will sit very tightly in the nest box until the eggs hatch. If mites are not dealt with and kept under control, both the chicks and the hen will suffer and, in extreme circumstances, may even die.

Always go through the routine of cleaning and spraying nest boxes prior to setting them up, even if they are new. Red mite are always present and are carried by wild birds, so new can never mean they are absolutely free from red mite! Use a recognised treatment and powder, repeating the process every few days to make sure the problem is kept under control.

Perching and Nest Boxes

Discouraging perching or roosting on or in nest boxes is extremely important, and preventing your birds from developing this bad habit will help to keep nest box areas cleaner and more hygienic.

Setting perches away from nest boxes is preferable, providing there is space to accommodate them elsewhere. This may not be possible in smaller coops where nesting and roosting areas may be adjacent. Keep an eye on the birds and encourage them to use the perches! Suitable spacing is essential as anything less will cause them to roost elsewhere, and nest boxes will be an easy alternative.

Separate Units and Roll-away Egg Trays

I mentioned these earlier and they are based on ones used by commercial egg producers. The birds lay the eggs and they roll gently away out of the cage and safely into a tray that is inaccessible to the birds. The nest box is fitted with a tray on the base that slopes slightly to the front of the box, so the egg rolls away under the perch at the front and into a tray situated outside the front of the box. The front of the tray usually has a lift up cover that acts as a double protection, denying hens, both outside and inside, access to the eggs in the tray. These boxes are usually made of moulded plastic,

A coop and run in urgent need of repair.

with no joints at all in the actual boxes, and any trays and perches are very easy to remove, making the whole unit simple and quick to clean and disinfect. The fact that there are no joints (joints are loved by red mite!) and the whole unit dismantles so easily makes protection against all insects easier, as they have fewer places to hide. However, plastic merely reduces the problem – it does not eradicate it.

These nest boxes need to be mounted on the wall in order to operate at their best, as this provides the correct angle for the roll away base to work perfectly. Some even come with folding perches, and these can be left down for easy access to nesting areas. If using such perches, ensure that the nesting areas remain clean.

The External Check

Once the internal overhaul of fixtures, fittings and bedding has been completed, the next step is to check the outside condition of your poultry housing. As with the interior check it is quite a simple task, but one that can easily be neglected. The soundness of the basic structure and the walls and roof will need to be checked and replaced or repaired as required. The proper operation of slide bolts and hinges is very important too – hinges can rust and break, bolts rust and do not fasten correctly, and this could allow Mr Fox a free meal.

Any windows need to move freely and should fit securely, runners need to be secured, and edges and runners must all be checked for red mite infestation. Pop-holes need to be strong and secure when fastened, and should open and shut properly.

> *Where the risk of fox attacks is very high, a security bolt fitted as an extra to secure the pop-hole is a very good idea.*

The roof of any poultry house needs to be checked for damage and wear. Roofs are usually covered with some kind of felt, and there is a real need to check very carefully for leaks and damage, and again to search for any signs of red mite infestation as they love to live and breed under the felt, which unfortunately has a tendency to split,

Roof felt in urgent need of replacement.

especially as the material hardens with age and becomes very brittle then starts to break up. What you often end up with is not only leaks but also a situation where a really strong gust of wind could lift the felt and eventually remove it completely, leaving you with a very wet shed and some very unhappy birds. Modern materials such as onduline and plastic are becoming increasingly common in recently manufactured housing, and both should last for many years.

Exterior Woodwork

Various types of timber are used to build poultry units today. Most are made from tongue and groove soft wood, but there is a tendency for people now to want the external timber for their poultry unit to be pressure treated. This was called 'tanalised' and ensured a longer life span for the wood. The problem is that with today's rules and regulations the use of certain preservatives is not permitted. The main one which has been removed is that old favourite, creosote. This had been used for many years in wood preservation, but we are not allowed to use it any more as it is deemed to be toxic and therefore unsuitable for use.

Today's treatments are mostly chemical-free and usually water-based. This means that any control offered by the earlier chemical treatments has effectively been removed, and also that there is now a need to treat wood at least once a year. The re-coating time for most of these products will depend on what the weather conditions were like during the previous year – the worse the weather, the more often you will need to re-coat.

A 'Wise' poultry feeder.

Check List

Remove all interior fittings.

Clean the nest boxes.

Clean all perches and any perch mounting brackets, and replace any perches as required.

Clean droppings boards (if fitted).

Check the security of any doors and windows, and any fittings securing them.

Check and repair any damage from rodent or insect attack.

Check and closely examine any cracks and crevices for red mite.

Remove *all* old and stale bedding and replace it.

Remove any cobwebs and dust from the unit.

Feeders and Drinkers

With the wide range of feeders and drinkers available today it has become a difficult decision as to which is best for your own birds and circumstances. The final decision should ideally be based on where and how your birds are kept, the number, and also which breeds you keep, with particular regard to both size and height.

> *With the rising cost of poultry feed today we also need to address every aspect of feeding to reduce wastage.*

Using the correct feeder will help to prevent the birds from flicking the feed out of the feeder tray, saving wasted food and therefore money, and potential hygiene problems, as any discarded food can become stale or attract vermin such as mice or rats. Keeping feed areas clean will help to prevent many problems and disease.

The wide choice available means that most requirements can be catered for with just a little thought and consideration. If you are new to keeping birds, the decision (as with housing, for that matter) should be made as soon as you decide how many birds and which breed you will be keeping – and well before they arrive. Factors such as whether you want to keep the birds in a free range environment or contain the feeding to the inside of the housing will of course make a difference too. The following suggestions should help you to decide which options are best for you.

Feeders

Feeders really come in three main categories; hoppers, troughs and tube-type feeders.

Hoppers are a great way of feeding larger flocks of birds as they hold a considerable amount of food. Normally they are large sealed feeders that stand on wooden or metal legs, and the fact that the feeder stands well above the ground makes it ideal for use in fields or on open ground. They are usually fully weather-, wild bird- and rodent-proof too. The feed is distributed through a central point at the base, allowing only a limited supply of food to be released as and when required. The chickens simply peck at the release mechanism and the feed is obtained, making them very economical. Although ideal for both outdoor and indoor use, they are usually too big for the average poultry keeper with a single coop or ark, as they hold up to 70 litres of feed, however, if you have the space they are ideal.

Trough feeders are probably the least economical in terms of wastage, and many are not suitable for use outside as they are usually open-topped. Those that come with a fitted top cover can be used outside, but due to the lack of protective cover provided by most, they are very limited in

Heavy duty galvanised metal drinker.

A 'King' heavy duty plastic feeder with rain hood.

protecting feed in bad weather. Smaller troughs can be used for rearing young chicks and growing on younger birds, as they are ideally suited for use in a brooder. The sizes vary from a very small chick size to some very large indoor units ideal for use inside laying sheds. Some come complete with an anti-spill grid that hinges or slides over the top of the feeder, and this will reduce waste. When choosing a trough feeder, make sure that any grids are a suitable size to allow the birds comfortable access to the feed, and always check to make sure they cannot be hindered or become trapped inside the grid, sometimes a concern when rearing young chicks and growers.

Tube feeders are now the most popular of all the different types due to their flexibility. They can be either metal or plastic, and free-standing or hanging, dependent on the design. Many can be used in every kind of environment too, as they are now often produced with all-weather protection hoods. These ones are *almost* weather proof, and the hoods can be removed if you decide to use the feeder indoors. Most tube feeders are very basic and consist of a cylindrical tube fixed to a round base into which the feed flows to replace any eaten. The tubes fasten to the base in a number of different ways – usually with a central pin or by means of a slot fit pressed into the plastic base. Many are also adjustable to allow control over the amount of feed allowed into the base feed tray, and even those that are not adjustable have a suitable setting for either pellets or mash to provide the correct levels of feed.

By using gravity to regulate the feed they allow food to fall into the tray as it is consumed, keeping it fresh and preventing waste. Many are now also fitted with an anti-spill grid that is either removable or incorporated into the base of the feeder, preventing waste. They are also almost all fitted with some sort of fastening that will allow you to hang the feeder from the roof of the poultry house. Wherever possible the base tray should be positioned at approximately shoulder height for the breed you keep – this will allow them to feed in comfort. Larger sizes are best for adult birds, but the single main drawback is that plastic ones in particular are easily knocked over if the breeds you keep are on the larger side.

Also available is a range of treadle feeders designed to be pest-, vermin and weather-proof. They require the participation of hens, but teaching them is quite simple; place something heavy on the treadle or lock the mechanism in the 'open' position for a few days, allowing the birds to get used to feeding from it, then remove the object or shut the feeder. The birds will continue to approach and step onto the treadle as they have been doing, giving them instant access to fresh, dry feed. They learn quickly, and if you have neighbours the inability of rodents to access the food is a great benefit. Most such feeders are metal, virtually indestructible and ideal for free range birds. The Grandpa's Feeder from New Zealand is probably the most well known.

Drinkers

Water is very important for a bird's health and welfare, and providing fresh water every day will keep your birds in top condition and allow them to live a healthy life. They can easily loose body fluid if denied access to a constant supply of fresh water and will dehydrate quickly if left without water, especially during periods of hot weather. If left for any length of time they could even die.

> *Having constant access to water is invaluable for correct growth and good egg production.*

Drinkers play a key part in any bird's welfare, and there are a wide range available for just about all requirements. Supplying drinking water in open containers is, however, not good practice as it gives free access to wild birds (a source of much disease) and the water will quickly become contaminated, especially during warmer weather when algae will develop rapidly. Using such a drinker could put your birds' health at risk.

Metal tray feeder.

This plastic drinker would benefit from sitting on a brick to raise it off the ground.

An 'Ascott' tube feeder.

As with feeders, drinkers with push and twist fit bases have taken over in terms of popularity, and there are many simple types of drinker which come with a basic tube which stores the water and fits onto a base using either a push or a push and twist action. They are usually clear topped so it is easy to see just how much is left, easy to use and clean, and cheap to purchase. For the small scale or garden chicken keeper they are ideal, and come in a range of sizes, usually 3, 6 or 12 litres. Most come with removable legs too, making them ideal for indoor or outdoor use, and virtually all can be hung for use in a larger coop or run.

For anyone with a larger number of birds there is now also a convenient and sturdy tripod drinker from Osprey which comes in 10, 20 or even 30 litre sizes. It sits on sturdy plastic legs and is ideal for heavy duty outside use, even on uneven ground when necessary, and comes with a removable clear plastic water barrel.

The other option is an auto-drinker which can save time and effort. They are mainly a hanging 'bell' design, but there are floor standing auto-drinkers too suitable for chicks and growers. They can be filled either by a mains water supply or from a separate tank and require only limited daily attention to confirm that the pipes and filters are all working correctly. The main problem occurs when temperatures drop and water supplies freeze – at such times it is advisable to switch off the supply and revert to manual methods.

One word of caution – larger drinkers can occasionally lead to sloppy habits. Your birds need a fresh supply of water daily, so do not be tempted by the lazy option of leaving it in a larger drinker for days as it will soon become stagnant and lead to health problems. Always change the drinking water regularly.

Wherever there is food there will be rats!

Vermin

When discussing the requirements for a healthy environment for your birds, it would be remiss not to mention the ever-present threat to both their (and our) health from rats and mice, and the threat to their lives from foxes, badgers and even dogs. We have already looked at the security of birds when inside the housing, but the problem does not end there. Birds inevitably attract vermin, both through the presence of their food in the garden or run, and warmth in the coop from their body heat – an ideal habitat in cold weather. In the case of larger predators, however, it is usually the birds themselves who are the food source.

> *Rats and mice are one of the most troublesome and damaging pests for the chicken keeper.*

All keepers are at one time or another affected by rats and mice. Both, especially rats, are very widespread, and although we rarely see them it is often suggested that we are never more than six feet away from one – perhaps an overstatement, but if it makes you wary then that's good enough! Rats are one of the greatest survivors on the planet, capable of living in a wide variety of places and conditions and, in common with red mite, will never be eradicated, only controlled.

The Dangers

By law we have to keep rodents under control because both rats and mice carry a variety of diseases. Rats were responsible for the spread of the plague, and there are many other serious conditions that these animals can transmit. One of the best-known in the UK is Weil's disease which is spread by rats urinating into water. Other diseases for which they are responsible include *hantavirus pulmonary syndrome*, another infection caused by rats urinating, *murine typhus* which is now a worldwide problem and spread in the same way as the plague (not directly *by* rats, but by a flea

Setting a rat bait station.

Various poisons are available. Some, such as Eradibait, are not harmful to pets.

carried by rats). There are many other different infections too which can be caused by rats for a variety of different reasons; via an open wound or by eating food which has been infected by rats' droppings or urine. Consequently contact, or even potential contact, with rats or mice is always better if treated with care and precautions taken when handling or cleaning any areas which have possibly been affected by them. Whenever there is any form of contact with rodents, always wear gloves and protective clothing.

Chickens are very vulnerable when it comes to rodents, and are especially at risk during the night while they are roosting.

> *It is quite common for a rat to kill and take a small chick or a young bird down into its burrow.*

Even small bantams are at risk and can be badly injured by a rat, with legs, feet and toes sometimes bitten off. Eggs are also easily taken and provide a very good food source for rodents, and feathers always make good nesting material, and can be taken directly from the bird, causing injury. This is especially common if a rat is making a nest during the breeding season.

Mice are a less serious threat, but they do eat and chew feathers while the birds are roosting. Many people who exhibit chickens will tell you that some of their show birds have had the ends of their tail feathers chewed, and this can obviously spoil any chances of a bird being taken to a show.

Both rats and mice will eat poultry feed, which costs you money, so you need to keep all feed in secure, rodent-proof containers. This should reduce the likelihood of a neighbour looking out of their window and spotting a rat running across

All this needs is a sign saying 'Vacancies' and it would be a perfect hotel for vermin.

your garden. They will also urinate into the food and drinking water, which creates a real risk of disease. The overnight removal of both feed and water containers is therefore good practice and should help to prevent rodent infestations.

Denying Access

All rodents are excellent climbers and that means getting into a chicken house is usually not very difficult – windows, gaps in joints, doors which do not shut properly, holes in floors and roof joints all make for easy access. During the day when the housing is open they can easily enter and hide. This means that when you secure the birds at night the rodent is locked into what is effectively a nice, warm hotel, without you even knowing they are there. The time just before dusk is when they are most likely to try and move in, and they will squeeze through the smallest of gaps, including places that you would never imagine they might get through. The small gap under a pop-hole will allow them entry, and if the gap is not wide enough they will often chew the area to gain access. Windows are also a good point of entry and need to be meshed. Always check in the corners and in nest boxes, in fact in all the nice dark places in the poultry house where they might hide. Poke around with a stick, and if they are in there they will most likely make their escape, making the birds safe for the night.

Detection

How do you know you have a rodent problem? There are certain things to look for, and although there are obvious signs such as recently dug holes around the housing, gnawing at the doors and pop-holes etc., you also need to check for droppings – mice leave lots of droppings which are small and black with pointed ends, approximately 4-6mm (¼ inch) long, and often found in groups. Rats leave shiny black droppings that are blunt at both ends and rather larger at approximately 12-18mm (½-¾ inch) long. They are usually more spread around too. Tell-tale signs on the housing may include small gnawing marks, scratches and tracks, especially visible in dusty dry areas, and there is usually a smell, because both rats and mice bring a really bad odour which is due in the case of males to their urinating to attract a female for mating purposes.

Raising the Housing

Poultry housing has for many years consisted of a shed sited on the ground. Larger units were occasionally moved and towed by tractors, but many were never ever moved, and this gave rodents an excellent undisturbed and safe hiding place below. Very large poultry sheds will always prove difficult to move, but all sizes of housing are better if they can somehow be raised off the

This hole is evidence of vermin.

Raising the coop off the ground will protect the bedding and roosting areas from vermin.

ground, and by fixing legs to poultry housing you can often immediately eliminate those dark, safe areas that rodents love so much – rats and mice do not like to be seen, and by removing a cosy hiding place it is far less likely that you will have problems with rodents in that area. They will still come for the feed, of course, and if they can climb up into the house they will, but by raising the unit it offers better protection and helps to reduce the problem dramatically. I suggest at least 25-30cm (10-12 inches) above the ground, and this should also give protection against other predators who also like a nice place to hide. A further bonus will be that the improved air flow around the housing will also be beneficial for both the birds and the longevity of the timber.

Modifications

Any existing poultry house can be made reasonably rodent-proof, but as the housing is open during the daytime it is virtually impossible to eliminate the problem completely. There must always be good ventilation in any poultry house, which means you cannot block every single hole as this would be very unhealthy for the birds. Fastening some really good strong mesh under the floor of the housing can be useful as it will prevent rodents gnawing through the floor, and if possible wrap the mesh slightly up and around the base to prevent them gnawing where the sides meet the floor. I have seen metal used as a pop-hole, and this is a good idea, but again the fit needs to be tight and snug.

Remove anything that gives a rodent somewhere to hide, including plants that are close to the housing, rubbish, piles of timber and anything else that may be lying around. Situate your compost heap well away from your chickens, and clear up any garden rubbish. Make sure that all feed and rubbish bins are rodent-proof, fastened and secure, and if you have any fruit trees or ivy growing up the sides of the housing this will need to be removed. *All* fallen fruit will also need to be disposed off as it will certainly attract rodents.

> *Site your poultry house well away from any fences and, if at all possible, centralised in the run to give good all-round vision.*

Poisons and the Use of Rat Bait

The fact that birds tend to spread feed all over the floor gives any rat or mouse an ideal opportunity for a free meal and there is therefore very little that can be done to prevent the occasional visit from unwanted guests, but precautions can and should be taken to reduce the attraction for rodents. A clean environment with no food left lying around will help, but it is virtually certain that at some stage you will have visitors, and then you must act rapidly to remove them as quickly and cleanly as possible. Poison, or bait, is one answer, and this is very effective and can remove them very quickly, but a word of caution – using any type of poison must be carried out with care and consideration for the environment and the surrounding area. Bait must be placed in areas inaccessible to other animals, birds and children and only in areas where you know there has been rodent activity. It must also be kept securely covered at all times.

Non-poisonous Bait

The easiest method is to put down rat bait, normally in the form of a poisoned wheat or corn, and this is very effective, killing them very quickly. The only problem with this method is that the body may not be found and will smell very bad until it has completely decomposed. There is, however, a product called Eradibait on the market that works on the rodent's digestive system and causes de-hydration, and although this tends to be a slower method, it will kill the animal, and also eliminate the smell of decomposition. The fact that it is both organic and harmful *only* to rodents also makes it a safer option for use around humans and other animals.

Traps as an Alternative

If poison is not the way you would choose to eradicate rodents, then trapping is really the only alternative, but whichever method you decide to use there is always the problem of disposing of the dead animal safely. Catching them alive is a better option for some people, and such cages are easy to set, but once you have caught them you still have the problem of what to do with the live animal.

> *Releasing them somewhere else is not an option, and in the case of a rat it is breaking the law. All you are doing effectively is passing on the problem to other people.*

Rodents are best disposed of in a quick and humane way, but if you do not take action the problem will only get worse. Impact traps kill as soon as a rodent enters the trap, and these are probably the quickest and most humane type available. They also remove the problem of disposing of a live rodent. I suggest using one which is ready to set as all you need to do is push down the back of the trap. In most cases they also come ready baited, which means you simply find an appropriate spot to set the trap, cover it up then wait for the results. Check out your local poultry supplier as they will be able to show you a wide range from which you can select the one you would prefer to use.

Preparing the bait box for work.

Setting a Trap

Traps or bait will not work if they are just left out in the open; they need to be under some form of cover such as a piece of wood leant against a shed, a pile of bricks, or anything that will both hide it and not attract other animals. By covering it you are creating a dark, safe place for a rodent to feel secure. If you have clear signs of rodent diggings and a hole, place the bait directly down the hole and cover it with a brick or something heavy. Always handle any bait or traps with care, wear gloves and make sure that any bait which you do not use is put somewhere secure and safe. Wash your hands thoroughly using a disinfectant cleaner afterwards.

The Fox

Of course the principal predator is the fox, but this is not the only predator; badgers and even domestic dogs can, under certain circumstances, be equally dangerous.

There is no doubting that the fox is a particularly attractive creature with considerable charm, but there is definitely a much darker side to this animal which farmers and poultry keepers will tell you about if given the opportunity. Beneath the façade is an animal that kills without compassion, and often seems to kill simply for the sake of killing. A fox will wipe out a whole coop of chickens and then perhaps take only one, leaving behind many dead and dying birds for no apparent reason. If this wholesale slaughter was done to feed the family and all the birds taken for food then the carnage might be more acceptable, but unfortunately this is usually not the case.

> *Birds are often decapitated and bodies strewn around the coop, and this carnage has been all too often the sight which has met poultry keepers' eyes first thing in the morning, and it is truly heart breaking.*

Breeding

The breeding season is from January until March/April, and during this season males will fight over females to gain the right to mate. Mating is a noisy affair but over very quickly, and a female may mate with several males, but will eventually settle with just one for the duration of the gestation period,

The fox – beautiful but deadly.

which is normally between 51 and 53 days. She will then produce a litter of cubs (kits) which can vary in numbers from 4 to 10. The male will supply food for the female up to and after she has given birth, but other than feeding he will leave them alone in the den while she raises the brood. Kits are born blind and do not open their eyes for about 2 weeks. It takes about 5 weeks for them to begin to explore their surroundings. The young foxes will leave the den in the autumn of that year and find their own territory, and as they reach sexual maturity at around 10 months it will soon be time for them to rear their own young.

A fox may live for up to 12 years, but the average lifespan in the wild is between 3 and 6 years. This varies considerably today though, as many animals are becoming urbanized, which means that their natural fear of humans is also disappearing. The ban on fox hunting could, however, cause some major problems for the fox population as hunting took only a very small number, but now the use of poison and shooting will probably increase the number of animals killed quite dramatically.

There is very little that we can do to control the breeding, but feeding them on the back porch is really not the answer – this is a wild animal, not a pet dog. I am aware that it is usually done with the best of intentions, and it is no doubt nice to see one in the back garden, but you are probably serving the animal with a death warrant. With the recent increase in back garden poultry it has no doubt given the fox an easy target as most people's gardens are not Fort Knox, and the temptation of an easy food source will always attract Mr Fox.

Other Predators

Although a pet and usually very friendly, a dog can easily become a threat to your chickens, and whilst some dogs will be quite happy and never bother the birds, others will want to chase them, and this alone can do serious harm to your birds. Dogs are essentially domesticated wild animals and natural

Buff Sussex in an electrified pen.

hunters, so always make sure that birds are quite safe when in contact with dogs.

Badgers are not normally a problem, but in remote areas they will go for an easy meal if it is available. Many farmers talk of badger attacks as being worse than those perpetrated by foxes, and I did personally witness a badger attack on a coop that held a small flock of Light Sussex bantams. The badger dug under the coop and ripped a hole in the floor to gain access. It then proceeded to kill the birds and was caught on camera walking down the driveway of the house, bird in mouth. The strength of these animals is considerable, so if you have badgers in your area, take extra precautions to prevent attack.

Birds of prey are not a major threat for most of us,

but there are certain areas where hawks can be a problem, especially for keepers of free range birds. Smaller breeds are more likely to be at risk, and prevention can be a problem as the only solution may be to house them permanently – not an ideal solution for a passionate free range keeper! Birds kept in a secure run can be given basic protection by hanging CD discs from wires above the pen which move in the wind and reflect the light, which is normally enough to put off all but the most determined bird.

Prevention and Protection

Most predators are opportunists and will take advantage of someone forgetting to lock the coop or getting home from work late. This is all they need to let them carry out a successful attack, so you have to be vigilant and try to make access to your birds as difficult as possible. Always be on your guard and never take it for granted that it will never happen to you. There are, however, a number of steps you can take which will help to protect your birds, but no way to guarantee that they will never fall victim to an attack.

Good quality wire fencing between 2 and 2½ metres (6 and 8ft) high and preferably leaning out at the top (foxes are apparently good climbers!) which is also sunken into the ground to prevent anything digging under the wire should prove effective in discouraging attacks. You will also need to dig a trench around the poultry pen about 30-35cm (12-16 inches) deep and about 20-25cm (8-10 inches) wide. The wire will need to be fixed into the bottom of the trench and along the floor before going upright, and laying the wire in this manner will certainly stop any digging. The wire at the base of the trench should be covered in rubble, or even broken glass, making it almost impossible for any creature to enter. Chicken wire will not be strong enough for this purpose, so a good, heavy duty weld mesh will be required.

Good catches and locks fastened securely to a strong part of the coop and electric fencing are also effective, but can be expensive. It is said that a fox can sense the passage of current through a wire, so electrification way well prove worth the investment if it prevents an attempted intrusion. As a very basic backup a single strand of electric wire might well prove effective, but taking all the precautions your budget permits together with a rigid regime of repair and maintenance would be my own personal recommendation.

A dog can be a very effective deterrent as a fox will usually try to avoid confrontation with dogs, and if one is roaming regularly around it will help keep

Electric strands shorting on straw.

> **" *Even a dog barking as a reaction to the sound of an interested fox will have a deterrent effect.* "**

a fox at bay simply by the presence of its scent. Even a dog in the house barking can deter an attack as a fox may just decide to seek out an easier target.

You could use a trap in the form of a large cage with a trapdoor at one end; this is a great way to catch a fox but what do you do with him then? It would be like catching the rat, but with a considerably greater problem of disposing of the live animal. If you want to try something really different then one old tale says that if you hang human hair near where the fox enters your land it will put him off. Human urine spread around the land and the outside of the pen will apparently also work as a deterrent to a fox, or so I am assured by a much older generation of chicken keepers.

The wiliest of all predators, and against which

Old English Game

there is little you can really do, usually enters on two legs. With the ever increasing popularity of poultry, and especially the more expensive show birds, you may possibly become a victim to this newest of poultry predators. Security lighting can help, together with strong locks and using smart water to mark any equipment. A CCTV system may also prove a deterrent, but wherever there is a ready market there will always be people prepared to supply it without the usual hard work.

Poisonous or Harmful Plants and Trees

There are a number of plants that are poisonous to chickens, but birds are usually quite intelligent and reasonably choosy as to what they eat, although you might not think so after they have wreaked devastation on an unprotected plant, or

Rhubarb – one of the common plants that are harmful.

one around which the chicken wire has become unraveled. Poisoning is, however, not unknown, so if we are going to provide a protective environment for our birds the least we can do is to guarantee that one of our own plants will not be the cause of their downfall. Some of the more common plants which are harmful to chickens are rhododendron, St Johns wort, rhubarb, horse chestnut, daffodil, laburnum, yew, buttercup, elderberry, both ivy and English ivy, hemlock, foxglove, hyacinth, lily-of-the-valley, tulip, wild onion, bracken (fern), clover and delphinium. I am often asked what plants chickens will not eat by frustrated gardeners, and these are probably the answers, although it would be foolhardy to test the idea by presenting a group of foraging chickens with the challenge.

Chickens need daily care and attention; if you cannot supply this then you will need someone who can look after the birds either on a permanent basis or in your absence.

They always need a constant supply of clean water and food and the latter *must* be kept dry.

Their housing has to be secure and predator-proof.

If you want a supply of eggs and do not intend to breed, then a cockerel is not required.

Housing should be moved on a regular basis to help keep the ground clean and fresh and free from potential parasites which could harm your birds.

The Welfare Code of Practice and several other regulations cover the keeping of chickens. These *must* be adhered to.

Brown Leghorn cockerel

Chapter Five

Handling Poultry

You will need to pick up your birds on a regular basis as this is the only way of checking them close up for problems, and by doing so regularly in the correct manner it will become easier as they become used to it. Every poultry keeper you will meet has their own ideas on how to carry birds, and most will differ slightly, but not greatly. As long as you provide a degree of support below the body effectively using one hand as a platform and the other to steady or calm the bird, or to keep the wings in check if there is a likelihood of the bird panicking, then you are on the right track. An alternative is to hold them in this manner but with the head held through under your arm – this position means that the bird is actually looking backwards. They remain very calm in this position as they feel quite secure. Ultimately your own choice of how to carry a bird will be determined by how comfortable *you* feel as you are doing it, and if you feel good then most likely the bird will too.

One important factor in how you might carry a bird is the actual weight of the bird concerned. Some breeds can be very large and heavy, and although these larger breeds are often docile and easy to handle, their weight will affect how you might hold them comfortably. From the point of view of both support and balance, using both hands is essential in the case of large fowl, whereas a smaller bird may simply sit on a flat palm once it is calm and comfortable. Rely on the bird to let you know if you are doing it correctly, and rest assured that if you are not doing it right their restlessness and attempts at breaking free will let you know!

Having the confidence to pick up your birds is essential for any chicken keeper as they will respond best if your actions are decisive and confident; any uncertainty on your part will result in them attempting to escape with wild flapping of wings which could hurt the bird and, in extreme circumstances, may hurt you – the sharp tips of a bird's wings have been known to inflict damage, usually to a keepers's eyes. Yet you will need to pick up your birds regularly. By doing so they will become used to it, and this will make your life considerably easier.

Catching chickens can sometimes be quite a task in itself. Certain breeds can be very active and flighty, and most of them will run away at a very surprising speed, especially if they feel cornered. If

If you are having problems catching your bird, try a landing net.

it is not possible to catch them reasonably easily, try using a large net – landing nets like those used by fishermen are ideal for the purpose. Another easier option is to wait until the birds go to roost in the evening as this is the time when they are at their most settled and relaxed, making them much easier to catch, reducing the amount of stress caused by the chase (both for the birds and for you).

As long as you keep chickens there will always be a need for you to catch them, and this is usually for close examination, but if you plan on showing your birds in exhibitions you will also need to spend time getting them as tame as possible. The more times you catch and handle them, the easier it will become, and this will save you the trauma of chasing then around the pen or garden, avoiding unnecessary stress. When it comes to night time you may well get the odd one that does not want to go to bed, but if tamed they will be easy to catch and put into the housing for the night – very important for their safety, especially if you are planning an evening out. It should, however,

always be done in a way likely to cause a minimum of stress and no injury, and should you become frustrated after an unsuccessful half hour of trying to catch a particular bird, take a break and let your frustration (and possibly anger) subside before continuing your efforts.

Catching and Picking up Birds

Birds that are not used to being handled will need special care. Try to catch them at dusk just as they are going to roost. This makes routine regular checks better for all concerned, and if it can be done even later when it is dark the birds will be asleep and almost in a type of trance. It then becomes a simple matter of picking them up off the perch which causes them very little stress. The only catch is, of course, the greater difficulty of examining them in the dark. If you are a keeper of a sizable flock you may well have electric lighting installed, but for the small scale keeper it will probably be a question of relying on garden lighting or the moon.

When catching birds during the hours of daylight, try not to make any quick or aggressive moves, and manoeuvre the bird (or birds) carefully into a corner where they will be easier to catch.

> *Sometimes a bird will crouch if you place your palm over her body, but it's not always that simple.*

If possible, catch a bird by holding the body from above and keeping the wings close to the side of the body, and without squeezing too hard. Try to keep the bird as upright as possible. Most birds will struggle and flutter at least a little and that's a natural reaction to being caught, but they will soon settle down when you get them in the correct holding position.

When you are trying to catch birds it is quite easy to try to grab the bird, but this is not a good idea as it is often the case that you end up getting hold of them by the neck or wings – this can in some cases injure or damage them. You may also end up getting hold of a bird by the leg or legs; if this does happen, hold it down securely then support the body from underneath before actually picking up the bird; this approach will always make a bird feel more comfortable.

For many years keepers carried chickens around by holding them upside down by the legs; this method is still in use today, especially in commercial poultry keeping and with some older keepers, and provides a way of carrying a number of birds at once without actually hurting them. Often at agricultural sales you will still see people holding several birds at a time in this manner, and athough it causes no harm to a bird if done correctly, this method is now often frowned upon. It is far better to carry them singly in a proper upright position, supporting the weight of the bird as you do so. Be

It may look 'odd' but the bird feels safe.

This bird has been handled from an early age and is completely at ease with the handler.

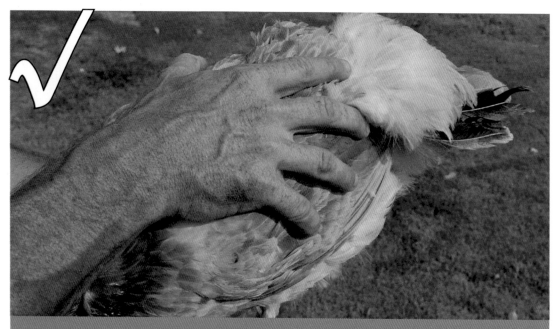

Whilst it may look slightly unusual, this position clearly works for both the bird and her handler.

especially careful if you are a beginner though, and always make sure you are holding the bird securely so that it has little room to struggle, but not so tightly that you might inflict damage. Most poultry keepers, after a while, both catch and hold their birds without giving it a second thought.

Becoming efficient at catching and handling birds is very important, but the level of difficulty you encounter can vary, depending on the type of breed you keep. Some breeds surrender and give up very easily while others can be more difficult due to them being very quick and flighty. As a rule the larger breeds tend to be more docile and it is usually the smaller breeds which prove agile and adept at avoiding capture, although this rule of thumb is often challenged by individual birds.

Catching Birds

If you have ever watched the movie *Rocky* you may well recall a training scene where the boxer chases chickens around a pen until he is fit and can catch them easily. This is definitely not a good idea, either for the owner or the birds. At least in

the film he did manage to win the fight, and in the case of catching chickens, so will you with a little patience and practice.

Catching birds can be an art form in itself, especially in the case of birds that are free range with either a meadow or a reasonable garden to roam in. If you cannot catch them later in the evening when they have settled down then you may have to take a little more exercise and do some serious chasing as chickens can and do move very quickly. Most chickens can fly but for the most part only over short distances, and if a wing has been clipped then this ability will be further reduced. A tame bird used to being handled regularly will not panic in your presence and will not be the least bit wary as you approach, but some birds can be a little bit wild or flighty, and if panic sets in as you approach the task can certainly become something of a challenge – let's just say it *will* keep you fit!

The best way to tackle catching a bird is to approach it very slowly and to try to get them into a corner. To do this effectively it helps to stand with your arms spread wide apart and walk *slowly* towards them. Although this may look a little silly to any onlookers it gives the appearance, at least as far as the bird is concerned, that you are in fact a lot bigger than you really are. It also always looks a lot less silly than sitting down red-faced and seriously out of breath.

Once you have approached and cornered your bird you will need to move quickly and decisively – take hold of the bird by the body and, as quickly as you can, support it with both hands. As already mentioned, if you do accidentally grab a bird by either the wing or the leg, change your hold *very* quickly to support it with *both* hands. Also, do not attempt to carry a bird by either the leg or by the wing as this can inflict damage – also no bird in its right mind will ever let you pick it up again! Using the two handed supportive position while occasionally stroking the bird's back will offer gentle reassurance that you mean it no harm.

Easy Breeds to Catch

It is very difficult to recommend a particular breed of chicken on the grounds that it will be easy to catch. There are always exceptions as all breeds can have some examples that make a mockery of any rules. One of the most easy to handle and tame though is the commercial ISA Brown, the normal chicken that you come across in commercial farms and the one you most likely have if you took in some ex-battery hens. Most ISA Browns are very easy to catch and will often stop and squat down, allowing you to pick them up very easily.

Many of the larger breeds are reasonably easy to handle and pick up – true gentle giants, in fact, and you just have to make allowances for their greater weight. Among the less taxing breeds are the Rhode Island Red, Light Sussex, Orpington, Cochin, Brahma, Poland and Silkie, all certainly some of the least flighty breeds available, although you will hear of exceptions.

Smaller breeds, and especially the bantam breeds, can be very quick and athletic, making the use of a net an easier alternative. These can be purchased quite cheaply from your local fishing store and are perfect for catching birds as they have a long handle which in most cases can be extended, or shortened for use in more confined areas.

If you are using a net then make sure you catch the bird without the outside metal frame ring hitting the bird. Keep the net low to prevent it from escaping, and as soon as the bird is trapped inside the net, hold it down for a few seconds until the bird stops struggling. All you need to do next is to carefully remove the bird without it becoming entangled in the net.

The Agile Breeds

More agile breeds such as game birds, Hamburgs and Leghorns are generally quicker moving and well known for their flighty behaviour. Bear in mind that this may cause some difficulty when it comes to catching and holding them, but do not let this put you off keeping any of these breeds as most are quite stunning and, provided you make allowances for their extra energy, you will soon master the art of catching and handling them. To base your choice of breed solely on ease of catching them would certainly be a mistake.

On no account catch your birds by the wing or leg. This can cause pain and damage.

Show birds need to be 'socialised' and used to people.

Washing your bird for a show would be impossible if she wasn't used to it from an early age.

Early efforts to get your birds used to people and being handled will pay off.

Done carefully, this bird is caught safely using a net.

A bird used to being handled will be easier to treat if needing medication.

For the experienced bird handler catching two smaller birds in a net is no problem.

If a lame bird is not used to being picked up its attempts to get away will add to the injury and distress.

Handling and Holding Birds

Once you have a bird securely under control, hold it with one hand with one or two of the middle fingers *between* the legs and the other hand placed on the bird's back, holding it reasonably securely but not too tight. This will make the bird feel secure and at the same time gives you full control over any movements. If you have a particularly active bird that will not settle down, hold the bird and wrap it in a towel or a similar strong cloth, making sure the wings and legs are all tucked in comfortably – this is ideal for doing any head examinations.

If a bird does not feel secure it will flap its wings and try to escape – a natural reaction for any animal if it feels threatened or frightened. This requires a degree of confidence from the keeper who must show authority and effectively convince a bird that he/she knows just what they are doing, means business and comes at the top of the pecking order – always an important consideration when dealing with chickens.

Holding birds can be a pleasing experience, especially once regular handling has helped them to become tame and friendly. This is very important, especially if you keep them as pets or have children.

Once in a box the chicken will become calm.

> *Calm, tame birds will always be more accessible to children and will help to encourage them to play a greater role.*

Chickens are very intelligent; in fact much more so than we give them credit for. Within the scope of their own small world their skills are very finely tuned and their abilities highly geared to their needs. They may have their limitations when they encounter some of the things we take for granted, but for the most part these things are irrelevant to a chicken. They very quickly learn where they live and soon develop habits that suit both themselves and their keeper, such as taking themselves off to roost as it gets dark. They know their position, their role and how they relate to their fellow birds and any people who they regularly encounter: this makes life much easier for all concerned.

A Word of Warning

When handling or catching birds always remember that they do peck. They also have sharp claws which can inflict injury, but the most likely cause of injury will be as they flap their wings in panic. Feathers are extremely sharp and can inflict injury to the eyes. Wearing goggles each time you pick up a bird may be a case of health and safety gone mad, but while showing confidence in your actions, never let it become complacency.

Carry Boxes

Travelling with birds over a long distance is always done better using a carry box of some description. These vary immensely in size and material, and range from rough and ready home-made creations to very sophisticated made-to-order designs, but they are ideal from the point of a bird's welfare while they are being transported. Some of the

Ever the opportunist – if a chicken spies a way of getting out, it will. Here Stevie McQueen attempts her Great Escape.

more extravagant options incorporate different sections to keep birds separate whilst in transit, and have almost the same sense of security for their passengers as a nest box. They are an essential piece of equipment for anyone showing birds and a pleasant alternative to having a loose and frightened bird creating havoc in a car.

If planning on buying or acquiring birds at a show, it is essential that you are prepared for it, either by bringing along a box or boxes, or by buying a box early in the day when they are still readily available. There are always a couple of people running around late in the day trying to relieve anyone and everyone of boxes for this purpose, and if you have not given it thought beforehand you may find that there *is* no box, or the one you end up with is just not fit for purpose. The familiar folding cardboard boxes are perfectly fine for show purchases and

cost at most a couple of pounds.

For anyone transporting larger numbers of birds, crates are the ideal solution and will carry quite a few birds safely, if not in luxury. Do not try to carry too many birds in a single crate or you will fall foul of welfare legislation designed to protect them from some of the cruel practices of the past, and you must make sure they have good access to both water and food whilst in transit, and also good ventilation. If you are either taking birds to show or to sell it will certainly be in your interest to look after your birds as it will increase their prospects for showing and will result in you getting a better price if they are for sale.

Light Sussex bantams

Chapter Six

Bird Watching

It is very important that you get to know your birds, and in many ways, the fewer you have the easier you should become familiar with their behaviour. Checking them daily will soon give you an insight into each bird's individuals character, and once you know them it will become easy to pick out any one individual who perhaps just does not look right for some reason or other. This should automatically lead to you investigating further to learn the cause of this 'out of character' behaviour. Trust me, chickens are creatures of habit and any one acting otherwise will have a reason – it could be something other than a health problem – perhaps the bird is simply eyeing up your veg – but by observing it you will learn more.

By observing your birds from a distance you will not be disturbing them, and this will give you a better overall view as to their health and fitness. If you are a newcomer to the world of poultry keeping it may take a little longer for you to recognise any out of character behaviour or potential problems, but you will soon learn and become very aware of what the general appearance of your birds should be.

> *Birds that are in any way ill or unhappy will show clear signs and these are usually quite easy to spot.*

Sick birds always look 'droopy', with lowered wings and a generally very unhappy demeanour. They tend to do little other than just 'stand' and do not move unless disturbed by something. That is why it is advisable to check the birds from a comfortable distance so that you get a true picture of what is actually happening in the poultry run as it is there that they will be most relaxed in the comfort of their usual familiar environment.

There is only one way that you can give your birds a thorough examination and in order to do this you will have to catch and physically handle each and every individual bird. To do this move slowly and subtly because once a bird is spooked it will be difficult to catch. Once a bird has been caught you will also need to be careful during the process of the examination.

This bird needs watching for early signs of illness - it has runny eyes and a pale face, indicating possible early signs of respiratory problems.

Handle them with care and try to avoid causing them too much stress. Consider how you would feel if you had to change places.

Chickens do not usually mind being handled, and become even easier to handle if it is done regularly, but there are exceptions. If a bird is hard to control, wrap it in an old towel – this will help to keep it (and you) safe, and should also reduce the chances of any increased stress. Handle them firmly and confidently, holding down the wings as these can cause injury, specifically to the eyes, if allowed to flap freely.

A sick Orpington chick.

A poorly Cochin.

around the neck too, checking the crop – the area directly beneath the chin where a bird stores its food before it is ground and digested. This can sometimes be a problem if a bird becomes crop bound, meaning that there is food stuck *inside* the crop which effectively means the bird is unable to digest any more food.

A bird should have a good strong red colour in both the comb and wattles and the eyes should be bright and clear. Breathing should be easy and light, and the bird should be clean around the vent area.

Common Signs to Look out for:

Birds looking droopy

Wings held low

Eyes closing or half-closed

Sneezing and gasping (or *any* breathing difficulties)

Runny eyes or nose

A generally hunched up appearance

Ruffled feathers and *any* signs of either feather or body damage

Any bird not eating (healthy chickens love to forage and eat!)

Any sign of blood

Observing from a distance will help to give you an overall idea of a flock's well-being and any birds which might be ailing, but many problems can only be seen whilst actually handling a bird. You are really looking for eye problems, runny noses and damaged or missing feathers. Check around the underside of the bird too, especially the vent area, looking for any swelling below. If there are any such signs then there will need to be further examination to check for any problems such as egg binding or any other internal problems. Look

Birds enjoying a Unipet foraging cake.

Chapter Seven

Keeping Your Hens Healthy – Inside

Feeding Your Birds

We all feed our birds every day but it often becomes a task we carry out without giving any real thought as to *why* we feed them the things we do. It is, however, a critical part of poultry management and the required welfare regime, as feeding the correct diet will not only keep the birds in top condition, but will also give the keeper the maximum egg production to be expected from the flock. Today's feed is rather hi-tech and scientifically formulated by specialist feed manufacturers to meet the complete nutritional requirements of each different type of bird, the purpose for which they are kept and the age at which they are at. It is a complete feed in itself, although treats and foraging are permitted, but only at certain times of day in the case of treats such as corn or wheat, which is best fed at the end of the day. It is very filling and will discourage birds from eating their normal diet of layers' pellets if fed too early. If fed late in the afternoon, however, it will keep birds satisfied overnight in the coop.

What has to be the main consideration for all poultry keepers is the birds' welfare, but also the cost of keeping the birds will have to be considered too – most of us do not have infinite resources. Feeding scraps of garden greens and veg may help to keep costs down, but it could adversely affect the positive effect of providing a complete feed, especially if given to the birds on a regular basis. It could reduce their intake of essential requirements, thereby reducing growth or making them more prone to ailments. To keep costs down it is better instead to avoid using feeders which result in a large amount of food wastage as this is definitely not a sustainable state of affairs economically and could encourage vermin – open feeders are the most wasteful, and hopper style feeders are normally the least wasteful, whether the larger intensive type for bigger flocks or the smaller screw fit type tube feeders which release food as it is eaten for a small number of birds.

Thanks to today's understanding of the nutritional requirements of livestock, the question of what to feed your birds has become a relatively simple one – if you have an adult laying flock then a good quality layers' pellet or mash will be ideal and is really the only responsible and sensible option. If you are rearing young birds then, dependent on

Top (left to right): Chick crumb and mixed corn. Bottom (left to right): Growers' pellets and layers' pellets.

health in very young birds. Also sometimes known as starter crumbs, it is fed as soon as the chick is dry, out of the incubator and into the brooder. The feed is in the form of a small crumb, making it easy for even the youngest of chicks to eat. The content of chick crumbs varies, but only very slightly, depending on the company supplying the feed. Feeding of chick crumbs is done from one day old till about six to eight weeks, but this may be variable according to the breeds you keep. Breeders of highly decorative breeds may keep chicks on chick crumbs for a slightly longer period before moving the birds onto growers' pellets. Depending on the manufacturer, chick crumbs contain between 17.5% and 19% protein and offer all the balanced diet a very young chick requires for the early rapid stages of growth. Amino acids are also present to help with both skeletal and muscle development.

When buying chick crumbs look out for 'ACS' marked feed. Products marked with these letters contain an anticoccidial additive as an aid to preventing coccidiosis, a killer of young birds.

Growers'/Rearers' Pellets

These are designed to follow on after chick crumbs. They should be introduced gradually to help the birds' stomachs cope with the change as they mature. They are normally fed from the ages of about six to eight weeks through to around sixteen weeks. Again they are a complete diet containing *all* the nutritional requirements for the age of the birds. The content of growers'/rearers' pellets includes a protein content of between 15 and 16%, plus 4.5% oil and 5% fibre. They also contain amino acids and minerals to help promote further growth and development. As with chick crumbs, the content levels will vary very slightly according to the individual supplier.

Layers' Pellets/Mash

Once birds have reached the age of sixteen weeks they are well on the way to maturity and 'point

their age, you will start with very young chicks from a day old on a chick crumb starter followed, as the birds mature, by a growers' pellet, finally moving on to the layers' ration, in the form of either pellets or mash.

As a guide to feeding your birds, the approximate average standard chicken, if there is such a thing, will consume about a kilo of feed per week; this can of course vary considerably depending on the breed and the size of the birds. There is also a wide range of feeds available to suit each stage in the life of your chickens, and right from a day old through to when the birds are in full production there is a feed designed specifically for that particular period of their life. Ornamental and show quality birds are also now catered for with a range of ingredients to enhance their appearance, ready for the show pens.

Chick Crumbs

Starting with the very earliest stage of the feeding process, day old chicks will require a chick crumb. This is designed to promote both growth and of lay', the period just before laying begins and when the body prepares for the process. There is no specific age at which laying does actually begin, but as laying birds reach this point they should be fed on a ration of either layers' pellets or mash. The typical age for starting to lay is 21 to 24 weeks, give or take a couple of weeks on either side. Layers' pellets (or mash) are designed to provide for a bird from this time and for the remainder of its life. There is little difference in the benefits of one over the other, with each manufacturer's product designed to enable a bird to both produce and remain healthy. It is therefore simply a matter of choice for the individual keeper. The average pellet contains 16% protein, 2.75% oil and 5.5% fibre, and the feed is a complete diet designed to include *all* the content required to keep birds in top condition, thereby also reducing the need for additives.

Breeders'/Show Pellets

Many poultry keepers exhibit their birds around the country or use them as breeding stock, and this requires a slightly different approach to feeding, with keepers looking specifically for improved fitness, feather quality, extra vigour and improved sperm and egg quality. After many requests over many years the feed companies have added products to their ranges designed to satisfy this demand for an extra special feed for these types of birds. They are designed to improve appearance through both top feather and body condition, and to do this the companies have enhanced the pellets with extra vitamins and nutrients such as omega 3 and other fatty acids, a higher protein count and extra amino acids, including methionine, all of which are ideal for extra fertility and improved hatching as well as improvements in condition and plumage. Farmgate supply a breeders' pellet, Fancy Feeds produce a breeder and show pellet and Smallholder Feeds an ornamental poultry pellet.

Finishers' Pellets

These are designed for the meat or table side of the poultry keeping market. They are designed to help produce the best possible type and quality meat bird towards the end of the rearing period.

When selecting a feed supplier check the labels for a list of the ingredients and any additives to make sure that they are for the intended purpose.

Corn and Split Maize

These are protein and energy providers and well loved by birds who will eat them from the morning onwards if given the chance, ignoring the more essential layers' pellets as they do so. They are very filling and ideal for keeping birds content overnight in the coop, so a small handful at the end of the day should suffice.

Grit

Grit is required by birds to be stored in the gizzard. It is then used to help grind up the feed to make digestion easier. Free range birds can and generally will find enough natural grit to give them an adequate supply for this purpose, although a modest supplement in feeds will still be useful. Confined birds do not have the same access to foraging and will therefore need to be supplied with grit in the feed as part of their diet. Corn with grit is readily available, as is grit on its own.

Mixing oyster shell with grit is a good idea as it gives the birds an extra supply of calcium.

Grit is now available from most suppliers and can be bought in a variety of sizes to suit most poultry breeds. Before you buy any do make sure the size of the pieces is suitable for your particular breeds.

Another feed option comes in the form of treats, usually veg, oats, corn or bread, but these should be fed only in limited quantities, if at all. The only other remaining feed is free, is enjoyed by most free range birds and consists of... well, just about anything and everything, from worms, weeds, prize veg and flowers to bugs and insects. A bird's keen eyesight will help it to spot just

Keeping feed sheltered from the elements is useful.

Hentastic 'Twist and Shake' forage feeder.

about anything, from bugs on a wooden fence to microscopic organisms in the soil. Chickens are undoubtedly happy foragers, but try to make sure that fresh layers' pellets are always available for your free range birds as they will not always find a balanced diet from nature, although they are usually well aware of which plants are bad for their health, and have their particular likes and dislikes.

These days it is actually illegal to feed your chickens on kitchen waste, and this specifically includes anything prepared *inside* the house. The intention behind this is to avoid cross-contamination which has resulted in the spread of illness such as foot and mouth disease in recent years and, although not specifically designed to affect small scale chicken keepers, it does include them. I am not aware of anyone ever having been prosecuted for feeding chickens excess porridge from a pan or lettuce from a bag, but that is the current position of the law, and as such it must be obeyed.

Treats – a Good or Bad Idea?

Treats are all well and good provided they are healthy and remain just that, and only in small quantities and not too often. Your birds might disagree vigorously with this point, but feeding treats can cause problems and may affect growth and health as well as egg production if given to laying hens over a period. It is, however, understandable that inexperienced keepers may believe that they are providing a treat for the birds, when they may in fact be helping to slow down the laying process or worse by feeding an incorrect and unbalanced diet.

Just like us, birds thrive on a balanced and controlled diet, and this is supplied by feeding the correct recommended feed – layers' pellets or any other generally available feed will contain the content to supply all that birds require for each particular stage of their lives. Feeding treats too often, or the wrong treats, will have an adverse effect on their diet, and as with corn, many birds will prefer to eat the treats and ignore the correct feed to their detriment.

Specially formulated 'treats' such as this 'Hentastic Cake' are available.

Acceptable treats for chickens could include certain fruits, vegetables, pasta or rice, but remember the point about not using kitchen waste.

Most people who keep chickens, especially today's garden keepers, do give them a treat of some description, and we all do it for the best possible reasons, believing we are doing something for our birds, but in actual fact many of the treats we supply have no nutritional value, and can in fact cause harm if fed constantly.

You can also buy treats especially formulated for garden birds. Uni Pet, for instance, have produced a herbal treat designed especially for chickens, supplying vitamins and minerals to help birds maintain good health. Hentastic comes in cake form to be fed in a feeder or as pellets to be distributed over the ground for birds to peck at as a foraging treat.

There are now a number of foraging cakes that allow chickens to peck and feed while keeping them active, and the benefit of these products is that they provide a balanced supplement to a chicken's diet based on a chemical-free herbal recipe whilst providing distraction for the birds.

What not to Feed

Avoid feeding the birds foodstuffs that are salty, sugary or fatty. Citrus fruit and meats are also not a suitable feed for chickens or any other poultry. If feeding treats, keep them to a minimum, and make sure that the treats you are feeding them have at least some nutritional value.

Access to Herbage

There are several common herbs that are ideal for chickens and you can grow many of them yourself in a small herb garden area. Poultry tonics often contain a range of these, together with

Nasturtiums contain natural antiseptic and antibiotic properties.

more general stimulants including garlic, onion, chickweed, dandelion, fennel, wormwood, rue, cleavers, cress, marigold, mint, vervain, comfrey, mullein root, thyme, marjoram, sage, nasturtium, goat's rue, guto kola and parsley. All of these are excellent for the general good health of your birds. A number of them such as chickweed and dandelion can also be foraged while walking the dog and fed fresh to the birds on your return – a healthy treat with zero cost.

Herbs and their Uses

Nasturtium leaves and seeds both have antiseptic and medicinal properties, and they can also be used as a natural wormer.

Southernwood, Wormwood, Mugwort, Tansy and Fennel can all be grown near the poultry pen as they can be used to control external parasites.

Other herbs with insect repellant qualities include rosemary, catnip, feverfew, lavender and pennyroyal. These can all be planted close by and as the chickens walk past or eat them they will provide some protection against certain insects. Spreading cut fresh herbs on the floor of the coop will also serve the same purpose, and they can be used as a food additive too, if required.

Comfrey is rich in protein and a very nutritious food that acts as a tonic. It contains high levels of calcium and potassium which provide a good source of amino acids. Chickens can be fed comfrey daily before the feed and this will help to keep them in good health and produce better egg yolks.

Chickweed is a very common weed which many chickens love and it provides a good source of greens for the birds.

Gotu Kola is perhaps less well known. It is a creeping plant which, if fed to the birds, produces a useful tonic effect.

Nasturtium is good for chickens as it is antiseptic and also has antibiotic properties. It is considered to be a good wormer too.

Nettles are always a good tonic herb for poultry as they are high in vitamins and minerals. They can also be used as a preventative against worms or dried and added to comfrey to stimulate egg laying. They are also very common around the garden as any gardener who has tried to control them will testify.

All of these plants are proven and perfectly safe to feed to your chickens, including many that you probably use on your own salads. A cross section of them fed to your birds will provide excellent health benefits.

my own experience I am convinced that using it in drinking water provides many benefits for birds — there is an improvement in growth and birds feather up more quickly. On birds bred for meat there is also a definite increase in both size *and* leanness of the meat. For me, however, the number one advantage is the fact that it helps with digestion, and although not actually a 'wormer,' it is naturally acidic and helps to control organisms, which do not thrive in an acid environment.

> *I have always used ACV with my chicks, right from just a few days old, and as soon as I know that they have begun to drink properly.*

In addition there is also evidence that it helps to reduce and prevent coccidiosis, and can prevent canker as it is toxic to the trichomoniasis protozoa. As a source of potassium it also helps to combat certain bacterial problems and controls levels of calcium, reducing the levels which form on the walls of blood vessels. Controlling calcium will also help to prevent problems with soft egg shells.

Adding cider vinegar to water.

Adding cider vinegar to water.

All Hail Cider Vinegar

Records of the use of apple cider vinegar (ACV) date back as far as 400BC. It has long been used for its medicinal benefits and is still today classed a one of Nature's wonders. It is beneficial for dogs, cats, sheep, cattle, and, of course, poultry, helping to reduce the incidence of some common infections and with the relief of both joint and internal problems. It also helps to reduce the frequency of intestinal problems, reduces odours produced by both animals and birds and there are even claims that it can help with arthritis in older animals.

ACV is rich in minerals such as potassium, sulphur, chlorine, phosphorus, iron and silicon. It also contains vitamins P, A, C, E B1, B2 and B6, as well as a selection of various beneficial acids. Through

Dosage and Usage

There is no exact recommended dosage, but I suggest using approximately 10ml per litre of drinking water, but not in metal drinkers as it will corrode them over time, eventually contaminating the water. As it is a natural product it is not possible to 'overdose' the birds, and if it is too strong a concentration they will simply refuse to drink. The acids in ACV will also reduce the growth of algae in drinking water. It is also possible to spray a *very* small amount over the feed to ensure that all your birds benefit from these properties.

Chamois (Buff) Laced Poland.

Other Uses

Damaged or bleeding areas on birds can be treated using a diluted solution of ACV. It will also help prevent many skin irritations, but if using directly onto skin it must be diluted at a rate of ten parts water to one part ACV. In addition it also makes an excellent equipment cleaner mixed with liquid soap and a small quantity of salt (for its abrasive qualities), and it is very good at clearing mildew too. Many older poultry keepers also still use cider vinegar to spray the insides of their poultry units, and this, I am sure, is due to its acidic properties, which make it an excellent natural fly and insect deterrent which will not harm your birds.

As a final point, ACV is also a very good cleaner of a bird's plumage, and a number of exhibitors bathe show birds in diluted cider vinegar to create a bloom on the feathers, and also to remove any grease from the plumage.

If ACV helps me avoid using normal antibiotics and other medicines, then it is not only better for the birds, but also for our own well-being. In my experience ACV improves the general health of birds and strengthens their immune system, which improves breeding prospects and enhances both feather and skin qualities. It is also readily available from most major feed and poultry suppliers, with some products suitable only for animal consumption, but there are certain products on the market which are intended for both human and animal consumption, and these are obviously the better quality product.

Regular Worming

Endoparasites (internal parasites)

An endoparasite is described as any parasite which lives *in* and derives nutrition *from* its host. Vets tend to refer to them using the general term 'helminths' which covers a wide variety of worms and internal parasites. They affect the internal organs of birds and include all species of worms and protozoa, including *Coccidian, Hexamita, Histomoniasis* and *Cryptosporidia*.

A great variety of helminths can infect birds. In free-ranging waterfowl, for example, there are many helminth infections with intermediate invertebrate hosts which in turn are eaten by the birds. Traditionally in both chickens and turkeys helminths have not been a major cause of disease or economic loss as indoor rearing prevents much access to intermediate hosts, feed is routinely medicated and birds in the broiler industry enjoy a relatively short life span. However, this is not necessarily the case today with the increase in the numbers of birds kept in free range conditions by smallholders, small scale poultry hatcheries and rearers and back garden chicken keepers. A survey of Ethiopian chicken production, where over 99% of birds are kept in gardens or backyards and allowed to forage, revealed the problem to be endemic, and although Addis Ababa is not Guildford, it will thrive here for the very same reasons it has there – access to intermediary hosts which curious chickens are ever keener to locate and consume.

Whenever birds come into contact with the droppings of other chickens or those of either domestic or wild birds, there is always a possibility of exposure to intestinal worms. Infection starts with eggs passed by one bird in the droppings which are then later picked up by other birds eating or foraging in ground that has become contaminated by droppings. The eggs can remain active in the ground and, once consumed, continue the cycle by hatching and maturing into adults inside the bird, eventually producing their own eggs which are then passed out in the droppings again. Whether or not problems will eventually develop in your birds depends very much on the balance between the challenge and the effectiveness of your control.

All birds are infected to some extent, but it is a question of managing the problem and keeping it below the point at which it becomes a problem for a bird.

Edwina Currie became renowned for her statement that *all* birds were infected. She was probably correct in what she said, but perhaps less correct in actually deciding to say it at the time.

Intestinal nematodes are the main type of helminths experienced by poultry breeders and keepers. There are three main types of significance and these are *Capillaria spp, Heterakis* and *Ascaridia*. Your vet will be able to distinguish them easily enough by the differences in size.

Roundworms (Ascaridia)

These are the biggest and the most common. The adults live in the lumen of the intestine but the larval stages invade the lining of the gut. They are white, up to 5cm long and may be visible in droppings in heavy infections, causing the bird to show symptoms of ill-thrift, enteritis (diarrhoea) and intestinal impaction. Severe cases can occur when there is a build up of contamination on bedding in the coop, especially if the litter is reused.

Chicken poo heavily infected with roundworm.

Caecal worms *(Hetarakis)*

As their name suggests, these worms spend most of their time in the lower end of the gut, the caeca (similar to the human appendix) and are common in chickens, turkeys and waterfowl. Frequently they are non-pathogenic, causing no obvious harm to infected birds, but they can carry another parasite, *Histomonas*, into the bird. *Histomonas* is the cause of blackhead in turkeys, and hence control of one parasite can help control another. It should, however, be noted here that *Hetarakis isolonche* can actually cause severe or even fatal intestinal disease in pheasants.

Hairworms *(Capillaria)*

These are the smallest of these nematodes but the most pathogenic when present in large numbers, the most common of which is *Capillaria obsignata*. *Capillaria* has a direct lifecycle (meaning it does *not* involve an invertebrate such as a snail or earthworm) and is most commonly a problem in birds kept on litter.

Another helminth that causes overt disease is *Syngamus trachea* and infection results in the condition known as 'gapes' in chickens and turkeys, but it can also parasitise the trachea of a variety of wild and game birds. A similar condition can be seen in geese but is caused by *Cyathostoma bronchialis*. Disease results from the physical blockage that occurs in the airway, leading to dyspnea or shortness of breath. The key clinical sign is an outstretched neck with an open mouth and a characteristic 'snicking' noise as the bird tries to clear its airway, but it can also manifest itself through poor body condition, poor feed conversion and ultimately increased mortality.

Although the lifecycle of helminths can be direct (i.e. involving just the birds) it is usually indirect with a cycle involving earthworms which can result in a particular section of pasture becoming infected for many years. Because of this fact, disease is most commonly seen these days in birds reared as free range or in outdoor pens. Endoparasitic disease in birds, such as infection with *Capillaria spp* or *Ascarids*, is more commonly seen in pens which are not regularly resited. It is important to remember that if disease (and especially 'gapes') is experienced in a pen then there will most likely be a high rate of contamination in the ground beneath it and disease could occur in any birds moved to that pen.

Worm infestations can be most easily identified by an examination of droppings for the presence of visible roundworms, although this will not help in the case of hairworms, which although more severe in their damage to bird performance, are actually too small to see with the naked eye. Alternatively, a routine examination of faeces for worm eggs can enable treatment before too much damage has occurred to the gut, or before any birds have begun to show ill thrift, lethargy and enteritis. Better results are often achieved by submitting any ailing, thin or dead birds to your vet for a routine post mortem examination and health screening, when visible and microscopic tests can be done on the gut. Of course there will be a cost to this but if there is a threat to the commercial viability of your enterprise it will be money well spent and will often highlight a problem before it becomes serious, i.e. if birds are pushing out large numbers of parasite eggs that could have been detected at an early stage in a droppings sample.

It is always a good idea to test the droppings of any new birds bought in soon after their arrival on site

Evidence of tape worm in chicken poo.

to confirm that they are worm-free, not only before they start to lay but also before you introduce them into your existing flock. Also establish a programme of worming with your vet depending on the number of birds you have, the species (i.e. if you have turkeys, worming should be a lot more regular to prevent Blackhead) and the amount of land available for them to roam. If you experience a drop in production, smaller egg sizes or a different shell colour then following this up with a droppings sample is always a good first move in ascertaining the underlying problem if no clear specific signs have been noted among the flock.

Even if no specific problems have been experienced, peak worm egg output will tend to coincide with peak egg production by your chickens.

Any sample taken at this time and turning out negative will give you certainty that there is nothing wrong. A sample taken late in the life of the flock also gives a good benchmark for your worm control strategy and lets you know the likely

Young pullets suffering from internal parasite problems.

status of that particular ground or paddock for the next flock. By routine sampling you will either confirm that all is well at that point in time, or you may uncover a lurking menace which you *need* to know of. At least in the case of the latter you will know what you are dealing with and will be able to do something about it before birds are lost or the egg yield drops dramatically.

Unfortunately there are relatively few anthelmintics (the general veterinary term for wormers) which are licensed for use in birds, poultry or game. *Flubendazole* (Flubenvet) can be given to flocks in feed to control intestinal nematodes and gapeworm, but unfortunately the dose rate licensed for use in poultry is not high enough to combat infestation with tapeworm – if tapeworm is diagnosed the dose would need to be doubled in order to deal with the infection.

Routine management control measures are essential and the best way in the long term of preventing worm burdens travelling between flocks or pens. Basic biosecurity is essential, and ensuring that litter is changed regularly and not re-used, as well as limiting a flock's contact with wild birds. All of these will help to reduce the risk of infection. Other 'homeopathic' controls such as mixing cider vinegar with the birds' water for one week in every four will help to alter the acidity of the gut and thus prevent eggs from developing into adult worms, although it will not treat an infestation that is already present. Regular monitoring will still be required too and is by far the best way of ensuring the ongoing health of a flock.

The presence of worms will be almost inevitable in laying flocks unless they are regularly monitored and treated or fortunate enough to be roaming 'fresh pasture'. It is important, whether you own a substantial number of birds or just a few backyard pets, to work with your vet and set up a protocol for monitoring the worm output of your birds. You should always remember to take into account the number of birds, the age of those birds, their access to wild birds and ground visited by wild birds and the amount of pasture or housing available before setting in place any worming plan.

Healthy Isa Browns.

Poo!!

Perhaps this might seem a slightly distasteful and strange subject to write about, but there are certain problems with poultry that can be diagnosed reasonably easily through the appearance of the birds' droppings. If you need a detailed diagnosis your vet will inevitably ask you for a droppings sample for examination; this is a standard practice carried out by most vets and can be extremely useful in determining if there is a problem and precisely what that problem is, so a cure or treatment can be started as soon as possible.

> *There are a number of basic problems that can be 'diagnosed' by an examination of the various types of droppings produced by your chickens.*

There are a number of basic problems that can be 'diagnosed' by examining the various types of droppings produced by your chickens. What you see will, however, often have many different meanings and causes, and there will also be times when this method may not necessarily give a correct diagnosis. For a definitive diagnosis there will need to be a proper clinical test carried out

Healthy droppings. The white markings are chicken urine.

by either a vet or a laboratory to confirm whether there are any problems which need to be dealt with. As an indicator the 'eye test' is, however, invaluable, if only as an early wake up call to a potential problem.

Normal Droppings

Describing what normal healthy droppings produced by chickens should look like will give you a general idea of what to look for when checking your birds. Under normal circumstances the droppings will be a reasonably solid blackish colour with an additional white crown; the black part is the solid waste and the white is urine. They should be quite firm, well formed and in an almost rounded shape. The picture above is an example of normal, healthy droppings, and if your birds are leaving these behind then they are most likely in a good and healthy condition.

Loose Yellow Droppings

Most poultry keepers are probably familiar with the custard like droppings seen quite regularly, and most back garden poultry keepers are probably sick to death of getting them on the carpet!

> *This type of droppings can be caused simply by feeding corn/split maize or greens, but it is also nearly always one of the main symptoms of worms.*

This type of droppings can be caused simply by feeding corn/split maize or greens, but it is also nearly always one of the main symptoms of worms. One of the other main causes of this type of dropping is respiratory infection; a problem which needs to be treated by a vet and can be easily cured with the use of the correct medication and prompt action. If you worm your birds on a regular basis then there should be no need for concern, but do be cautious because even though you may have wormed them, it is still very easy for them to pick up further infestations during their

Sometimes funny looking droppings are simply a result of what has been eaten.

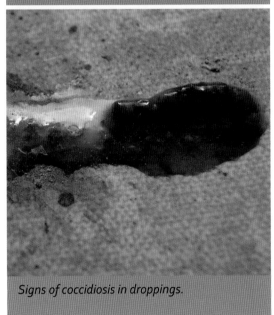

Signs of coccidiosis in droppings.

Coccidiosis

Not in itself a type of dropping, but as this is one of the most dangerous of all problems which can be observed in the droppings, it is certainly worth a mention. The internal parasite responsible is always more common in young birds which have not reached full maturity, normally between 6 and 12 weeks. It is during this period when the birds seem to be at their most vulnerable. The signs are usually very clear to see, and in most cases there is a cure if the problem is caught at an early enough stage. The birds will become lethargic, their wings will droop and they will stand with their heads down looking clearly unhappy. Always check the ground or floor below where the birds roost, and fresh shavings on the shed floor will soon show up any problem droppings as they stand out extremely well on clean shavings.

If coccidiosis is present the droppings will have a bloody red appearance, and when examined the droppings will contain what look like small jelly-like worms which are red in colour.

When this stage of infestation is reached the problem is well established and losses may well follow, but at this stage do not separate the birds, but under no circumstances mix them with any others from different pens or coops. All the birds in the infected pen will need the same treatment; an oral dose of an anti-coccidial treatment such as *Amprol* which must be obtained from a vet and given to the birds as soon as possible. It will be necessary to dose every bird in the pen to both stop further infection and treat the remaining birds which will most likely also be affected. The other birds in the same area would no doubt soon

daily routine, especially if left to forage. Try to keep a close watch on them and if the symptoms persist and worming has not controlled the problem, then a consultation with the vet is definitely recommended.

Droppings showing signs of worms. Note the red jelly in the droppings.

will seem both droopy and pale, and there will most likely have been a drop in egg production. I recommend administering a good quality wormer in accordance with the manufacturer's recommendations on a regular basis. The one I use under prescription is *Panacure* which is mixed in with the drinking water. The treatment is over 4 or 5 days, but is very easy, economical to use and avoids more expensive problems at a later date. There are in fact quite a few treatments on the market that come in either tablet, powder or liquid form, so the choice is up to you. Flubenvet and Verm-X are the most popular and familiar brands available today and are both readily available and easy to use. Ask your local poultry supplier for more information as to which will best suit you.

White at the Vent and with Light Green Droppings

Again there are probably various causes and it is sometimes nothing more than diet.

However one possible cause is too high a protein content. But in most cases the problem is likely to be more deep rooted. I have found from experience that once a pale green fluid appears there is already a very bad internal infection, and sadly the results are often fatal. Older books written prior to the heavy regulation of medicines recommend using Epsom salts and various other concoctions, most of which are now either unavailable or even illegal, so I simply try and keep the birds separated and as comfortable as possible, with a constant supply of fresh water containing a small dose of cider vinegar, and I also worm them orally using a syringe as a back up. I have had some success which makes the effort worthwhile, but I must admit the results are not very impressive.

have picked up the worm as they were pecking round in the pen – transmission is both very easy and very quick.

One small point to remember is that this disease can be easily transmitted from bird to bird, but also by us carrying the problem on our feet, or more precisely on our boots and shoes. During a period of infestation extra vigilance and cleanliness is needed, and not just in the coop but also from you, the keeper, who is the main link between the flock and consequently the most likely carrier! It is not overstating the matter to say that if the *coccidiosis* worm is not treated it will kill – birds will certainly not be able to recover from this problem without outside assistance.

Normal Worms

Although these are not as serious as the previous worm, they do require treatment and keeping under control. It is precisely the same procedure as with the family cat or dog, which also need to be wormed. The signs are quite easy to see — liquid yellow droppings, some of which actually contain worms which may still be moving. An infected bird

The main consideration when dealing with *all* types of internal problem is that they are caused, in most cases, by an infection from the ground on which the birds roam and that infection was probably carried either by other birds or by us.

As a preventative measure cleanliness is the

single most important factor in protecting both ourselves and our birds – use disinfectants, foot baths, clean fresh feed and, most importantly, good clean bedding which *must* be changed on a regular basis. This type of good management always gives good results and will in the long run save you considerable time and money.

In every respect, prevention is always better then cure.

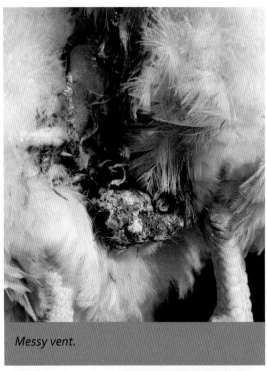

Messy vent.

Poo check - early warning signs	
Chickens from 0 to 12 weeks	
Vent pasting	The chicks are too warm or too cold
Watery diarrhoea	Possibly enteritis or anaemia
Bloody diarrhoea	Blackhead, coccidiosis or enteritis
Growing to Mature	
Watery and bloody	Coccidiosis or thrush
Yellowish droppings	A respiratory disease or worms
Green to yellowish	Internal problems

These are some very basic and simple checks to make, and although not up to the level of a proper analysis they will tell you when to perhaps be on your guard. Do be aware, however, that the food you are giving, the environment in which they live, and many other factors can contribute to the varying appearance of droppings. Do not panic if droppings look irregular or different from the description of 'normal and healthy', but if you do have any concerns, contact your local poultry vet for good sound advice as to what to use and what to do regarding the welfare of your birds.

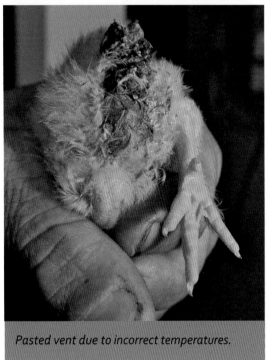

Pasted vent due to incorrect temperatures.

To treat impacted crop, try gently getting cider vinegar down the bird's throat.

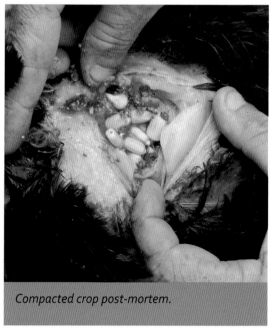

Compacted crop post-mortem.

Crop Bound

This is also known as impacted crop. The crop becomes enlarged and the birds cannot eat or drink. In most cases they will appear to be unhealthy and probably hunched up. Grass is normally the main cause of this condition, so prevention can be quite difficult, especially if your birds are allowed to roam over grass or there is grass within the run. Try not to allow the birds access to grass cuttings and long grass, if at all possible.

In some cases you can treat the problem by using either cider vinegar or warm olive oil and pouring them down the bird's throat, then massage the throat very gently, making sure there are no sharp objects trapped in the crop. After about 15 minutes you should be able to hold the bird slightly downwards to remove some of the solid matter. If the blockage shows no sign of moving then it may be a case of taking the bird to the vet and having it removed surgically.

Gently squeezing out the fluid.

Left and right: a chicken showing a very visible and severe case of sour crop.

Sour Crop

Sour crop is very easy to diagnose – you will notice a very bad smell coming from the bird's mouth. Once you have smelled it you will certainly never forget it. Any birds affected will become lethargic, look very droopy and most likely have a noticeable swelling below the breast. Unless it is treated the condition will almost certainly deteriorate.

Treating Sour Crop

To treat sour crop start by holding your chicken upside down with the head away from you and gently massage the crop from bottom to top so that the fluid is eventually released. You may well wish to do this out of view of any neighbours who may not understand your reason for holding a chicken upside down! Once this has been done, mix some natural (live) yoghurt into the layers' pellets or mash and feed this to the bird, along with water mixed with apple cider vinegar throughout

the day. You will probably need to repeat this over three days until the crop stops filling and the bacteria in the crop return to normal. If the problem persists for more than a week, seek a vet's advice as a course of anti-fungal medicine may be required.

Avoiding Sour Crop

In order to avoid *any* crop problems you should make sure that there is an ample supply of grit together with the birds' supply of pellets. Grit breaks up the food in the crop and without it the food cannot be broken down and digested. The calcium in the grit will also benefit laying birds.

Long grass should be cut down too as this can compact in the crop, and any stodgy foods such as bread and pasta should be fed sparingly as treats as these can also cause compaction in the crop.

Prolapse.

Prolapse (an Egg Layer's Problem)

A prolapse is very easy to spot; the bird's vent area will become very messy indeed, and in many cases the bird will produce a large amount of white droppings. The bird's actual oviduct will protrude from the vent in what can only be described as a 'bloody mass'; what has happened is that the oviduct has turned itself inside out, which then causes the egg to be trapped inside the sac. There is little chance that the hen will ever be able to pass this egg without help. Once a prolapse has happened, steps will need to be taken to replace the oviduct back inside the bird — this needs to be done as soon as possible to try and prevent the problem recurring and also to prevent infection.

Symptoms

The first and main symptom you are likely to see is that the bird seems to be having problems laying her eggs, resulting in very frequent visits to the nest box to try and lay. The bird will suffer if left unattended in this condition, but if the actual egg sac is not visible on the outside of the bird, put her in a seclusion box or a quiet space and keep her as calm as possible. Feed her on a light wheat diet and she may at this stage possibly part with the obstruction herself. If, however, there is a visual appearance of the egg sac then the matter must be dealt with, as this is the decisive symptom and calls for immediate attention.

Ways of Preventing the Problem

One of the main causes of a prolapse is the chicken straining to lay eggs, or in the case of some commercial layers, producing too many eggs too soon. It is not uncommon for birds to be fed a ration to help produce eggs as early as possible, and to do this a diet to stimulate egg production is often used, especially during the winter months. There is no real harm in this type of rearing, but there are certain birds who may be adversely affected by this type of feed, with the result that they either lay before they are ready, or lay eggs which can be far too large for their own comfort.

With such exceptionally large eggs it can and does cause excess strain on the birds. This in turn can cause an inflammation of the mucous lining, the inflammation then adding to the problem of passing an egg which is really too large to pass through the system normally. The extra pressure the bird uses to try to lay the egg then effectively turns the whole internal sac inside out, and this is what becomes visible from the vent as the problem develops. There can be other reasons for a prolapse, one of which is the bird being constipated. This will present precisely the same symptoms as those caused by a large egg.

There is no guaranteed way of preventing this problem, but it will help not to overfeed your birds on high egg production feeds.

If you have a bird or birds with a prolapse or any of the early symptoms, remove them from their normal high protein layers' diet and feed them lightly on corn/wheat instead with a few added vitamins until the birds are recovered and ready to go back into production. You will need to check them on a daily basis, especially any classed as point of lay pullets, and keep up the checks until they are around six months old. Ideally all birds should be checked daily as one of the principles of good poultry management.

Although I have on occasion seen a few prolapses in older birds, this is very rare and it is almost always a problem of birds in the early stages of laying, or when beginning to lay once more after a period of non-laying such as the moult.

Egg Removal from the Oviduct

Once the oviduct is visible outside the vent, the very first step is to make sure that the internal sac, which is now on the outside, is kept very clean. I suggest you try to get someone to help by holding the bird while you attempt any repair. The oviduct can be held gently, but do not squeeze it. You can then gently pull back on the skin until you see the end of the formed egg inside the sac. Continue to pull back very gently on the skin – although it may be a little tight it *will* slide back over the egg. There will be a slight amount of bleeding, but this is usually not a problem.

In many cases the egg is very visible, but if this is not so then do not be put off – just keep looking; there is definitely an opening there somewhere.

It may help when attempting to remove the egg to use a little Vaseline both in and around the vent and sac area to lubricate the skin.

You must take great care not to break the egg when doing this. If there is an accident and the egg does break then you will need to use your fingers to clean out *all* the bits of broken shell, making sure there are no bits left anywhere inside the oviduct and that it is left very clean. If any bits of the broken egg are left inside the bird, it is virtually certain to cause an internal infection *(peritonitis)*, which may well result in the bird dying. Make sure that any disinfectant you use to clean the egg sac is bird friendly and mild, and not just something from under the kitchen sink. Barrier V1 is perfect for this type of cleansing.

Treating a Prolapse

Once the egg has been removed from the sac and any protruding parts thoroughly cleaned, the remaining treatment is relatively simple and can be done by most keepers themselves. The main requirements are patience combined with time and effort. As soon as you become aware that a bird has had a prolapse she will need to be separated immediately from the rest of the flock. If you do not separate her, the other birds are highly likely to peck at the protruding parts, and once they get a taste for it there is usually no stopping them until the victim is dead – not a nice fact, but unfortunately a very true one.

As always, one of the main considerations must be hygiene – once the oviduct becomes visible there is an immediate need to keep the flesh clean. If necessary wash and clean the sac.

The bird is now very vulnerable as it is very easy for her to pick up an infection if treatment is not carried out very quickly, in the same way an infection might gain access to an open wound. You must push the oviduct back inside the bird, making sure you do not tear the sac. To do this put some Vaseline onto your fingers and gently guide the sac back inside the vent. Try not to do it with sharp nails as this can do considerable damage to the bird's insides while you are pushing the prolapse back into place. Once you have the protruding sac back inside the bird's vent, push your finger well inside to stretch out the sac into a reasonable position.

Once the sac is back inside the bird you will almost certainly find that the process has to be repeated several times until the oviduct finally stays in place on its own. I always use a haemorrhoid cream (the one that people use for piles), and this not only disinfects but lubricates, as well as helping to shrink and tighten the oviduct. This is a method that definitely works, and with good results too. Once the bird has been treated she will need to be kept on her own until she has improved and healed enough to be moved back in with the flock.

If this treatment is carried out with due care, the success rate is quite good. The picture vividly shows the problem, although unfortunately the bird concerned was already dead when the photograph was taken. In this case the owner had no idea what the problem was until it was too late. The main cause of loss is the egg sac being on the outside of the bird, which very soon becomes infected, and it is this infection which usually proves fatal.

Life after a Prolapse

Once a bird has suffered a prolapse there is always a possibility that it may occur again. This is not always the case though, and I have had birds live and lay quite normally for many years after recovery. I would recommend that you keep the bird on a diet which will limit its egg laying production for as long as possible. A light diet of wheat or corn would be ideal, and by doing this it will give the bird enough time to heal properly and any internal damage to return back to normal.

There is always a possibility that in rare cases a bird may never lay an egg again. If this is the eventual outcome then you will have to consider whether you treat her as a very nice pet or dispose of her. It is a decision that at one time may have to be taken by any chicken keeper.

Treatment by a Vet

If after reading this you decide that you cannot handle the situation but you really want to try and save the bird, then the local vet is probably your one available solution. The vet will push the egg sac back into position and then sew across the vent to hold in the oviduct. This does work in most cases, but there is a reasonable possibility that as soon as the stitches are removed the bird may prolapse again. This is because the oviduct has been held back in place by the stitches, and these do not help the prolapse to strengthen up and stay in the correct position on its own. If you treat the prolapse in the way I have described, the bird will build up its own strength, and the repair will be more permanent and more successful. Recovery does take time but it is quite surprising just how quickly a bird returns to its normal routine.

Do not let problems such as a prolapse put you off keeping chickens. Whatever animal or bird you keep can and will become ill at some stage in its life, so just carry on and learn by your experience.

Egg Bound

Hens and pullets can be susceptible to a condition known as 'egg bound'. This is when a bird has either a part-formed or fully-formed egg which is stuck or restricted inside the bird. She then finds herself unable to lay or remove the obstruction, which can cause severe discomfort and even loss of life in extreme circumstances. There are several causes of this complaint, ranging from very large eggs and vitamin deficiency to contraction of the oviduct. The condition can be corrected when it occurs, but most importantly it can be prevented too through correct care, diet, breeding and management.

Egg bound is a reasonably common problem and affects many poultry breeds and a large range of other types of birds too. Chickens, however, are at the greatest risk of encountering the problem due to their constant egg laying. The results can be very serious for a bird's health, and can also cause a considerable amount of lost production. There are a number of different treatments, but they need to be administered carefully.

The actual cause of the problem is usually the egg becoming stuck inside, near the *cloaca* (vent) area, or sometimes even further back inside the bird. Once the egg has become stuck in this position it can be very difficult to release it easily, and this is where care must be taken as the condition can lead to infection and damage to the birds internal tissue in the same way as a carelessly treated prolapse might.

> *The problem is commonly spotted by the sight of a bird being 'hunched up' with its tail down and looking very sorry for itself.*

Applying haemorrhoid cream to the vent area.

Pushing the cream gently into the vent.

Pick the bird up and it should be easy to feel the lump inside her – it may well feel solid and fully formed, which means it must be removed as soon as possible.

Treatment, if it can be called that, can be done by administering very gentle massage to the area where the egg is stuck. Let me stress at this point that although you can feel the egg inside, you must be careful not to put too much pressure on it! This massage may, in some cases, allow the egg to be laid as normal. What you must try to avoid is breaking the egg inside the bird, which is very easily done. As with the prolapse, if the egg breaks inside you will have to make sure that any particles of egg and shell are removed to avoid infection. To remove all the shell particles means that a thorough cleaning of the oviduct is required; this is easily done by gently inserting your fingers inside the vent and removing all the debris.

If massaging fails and the egg is still stuck, dip your finger into some Vaseline, petroleum jelly or other similar lubricant and then insert it as far into the vent (cloaca) as possible. You will more than likely feel the tip of the egg, so lubricate the vent very well and also the end of the egg that you can feel. This extra lubricant may just help her to pass the egg normally, but you can also gently push down the abdomen of the bird in an attempt to move the egg closer towards the vent.

The use of a warm fire or steam as a heat source is an old method which has been used for many years. Hold the bird in front of the fire to warm her rear area for about ten minutes; this should result in the bird laying the egg, which means she may be back to normal. The alternative is to use steam by holding the bird's vent area over a jug of steaming water. This should have a similar effect to the fire, with the heat helping the bird to lay the egg naturally. When using these methods you must remember not to hold the bird *too* close to the heat source as to cause discomfort – leave enough space to allow the bird to warm up, but not to get overheated and stressed.

If none of these methods achieves the desired result then you may well have to break the egg while it is still inside the bird. As already emphasised, you must be completely sure to remove *all* the broken particles and egg in order to avoid infection. Breaking the egg is the very last resort when all else has failed, and this needs to be carried out very carefully to try and avoid damage to the internal areas and the vent.

Once the egg has been broken, take time to gently clean out the area. This is quite easy to do and, although not very pleasant, it is not as bad as it might seem at first. Once you have removed all the fragments, wash out the egg sac using a suitable mild disinfectant or similar solution as before to try and avoid any infection.

There can be a number of different reasons for this condition, but the most popular explanation blames a lack of calcium or phosphorus, both of which are needed for egg production. There could also be the simple problem of eggs which are just too large or possibly deformed. This happens by using birds which are both too young and too small in the breeding pen. A lack of proper nesting areas can also be to blame as it may cause a bird not to want to part with the egg due to the conditions – this situation is referred to as deliberate egg retention – simple but true. Stress, improper husbandry and hormonal balances could all be wrong too and these need to be taken into account as a possible cause when reviewing your management regime. If any management practices are found to be at fault then correct them right away.

Spotting the problem can sometimes be quite difficult as some birds are very good at hiding illnesses. Look for birds which are low and appear depressed; the tail may be held down and the bird continually straining the abdomen to try and dislodge the egg. There will also most likely be numerous visits to the nest box which obviously produce no results. The abdomen will be distended too and the bird can become very cold. If this does happen it always helps to get the bird into a warmer environment or even under a heat lamp until the problem has been solved.

The risks when treating this problem are high, and this is why I have stressed the need for care. If done incorrectly the removal of the egg can cause peritonitis, bacterial infection and even secondary infections which can ultimately result in fatality. If after several attempts there appear to be no signs of improvement it is perhaps time to consider the bird's welfare and the likely suffering these infections may cause her. It is a difficult decision, especially for the small scale and back garden keeper when a bird is more akin to a pet, but we are not talking of commercial considerations here, but rather the suffering a bird will experience. Sometimes such decisions are simply unavoidable and have to be made for the better good of a bird.

Vitamins Required for Healthy Chickens

Fat-soluble vitamins

Chickens need to ingest certain vitamins with fat in order for the vitamins to be properly absorbed into the bloodstream. Vitamins A, D, E and K are necessary for chicken fertility and the production of strong eggs.

Water-soluble vitamins

Chickens, like all life, require water to survive. The water-soluble vitamins that chickens need are thiamine (B1), riboflavin (B2), B6, B12, pantothenic acid, choline, folic acid, biotin and niacin. The water-soluble vitamins help with the chickens' growth and egg production.

Minerals

Chickens require minerals for egg production, bone development, muscle function, metabolism and the formation of blood cells. The most important minerals are calcium and phosphorus, which are essential for the formation of strong, healthy eggs. Chickens also require trace amounts of minerals such as salt, copper, iron, manganese, magnesium, iodine, zinc and cobalt.

Adding vitamins to the feed.

lack of calcium in the diet. Remove any corn or maize treats and feed the bird (or birds) on layers' pellets/mash together with a grit and oyster shell supplement. A tonic or multi-vitamin treatment will also help. Providing a source of calcium such as yoghurt is popular with older keepers, but remember the rules about feeding kitchen waste.

Soft-shelled or malformed eggs

Finding misshapen or odd-sized eggs can happen at any time, but if the problem keeps happening then the cause needs to be ascertained and appropriate action taken. Rough or crinkled eggs are generally caused by a problem within the chicken's oviduct and the cause can be that she is laying too heavily or being fed a feed that is causing her to 'force lay'. Extra green stuffs in the diet can help to rectify this problem. There are, however, occasions when the problem may be passed on through a chick as the result of a genetic problem.

Soft-shelled eggs are most likely caused by a

Eggs are sometimes produced with flat sides and these can be the result of an over fat hen, with the layers of fat pressing against the egg as it is forming and affecting the shell as it hardens. Eggs showing signs of pimples are normally the result of a hen starting to lay again in a new sequence after a break. Small or tiny eggs are normally the result of very young birds coming into lay. These eggs are usually shelled around just the white with no yolk. This can also be the result of a bird coming into lay before she is really fully ready to do so. Any birds coming into lay too early will inevitably produce eggs with various inner and outer faults as their bodies mature.

Brahma

Chapter Eight

Problems with the Comb, Wattles and Head

Normally a bird's head is primarily a displayer of symptoms rather than a particular source of actual health problems. Anything other than bright eyes, clear nostrils and good red combs and wattles is often indicative of an ailment, but usually in a different part of the body. If the comb appears to be paler, darker, going a purple colour or generally looks unusual in appearance or colour, it could be a sign of illness. There are many examples of this in the section dealing with internal problems which are by far and away the biggest problem birds encounter as natural foragers.

The main problems actually affecting a chicken's head usually concern the comb and wattles, as they are easily susceptible to injury and damage. Certainly the weather does affect them, with frostbite always a possibility during winter, and the other problem likely to affect combs and wattles is conflict between birds in the flock, especially cockerels, which have a tendency to fight when together. The only other likely areas of conflict are when a new bird is introduced into an existing flock, or if a bird is being bullied which can on

occasion be extreme. As a conscientious chicken keeper these should be signs you are looking out for every day, and where you do see signs of damage, take action by finding out which might be a troublesome bird and which is a victim, and then take action by separating them appropriately, and treating any damage promptly with antibiotics.

Cold Weather and Frostbite

During spells of very cold weather when temperatures go well below freezing, the birds' combs and wattles can be very badly affected and can suffer from frostbite. This is not uncommon in birds that are left to roam outside, especially when there are early morning frosts and the birds emerge from a relatively warm and sometimes damp coop. Any birds that are affected will show clear signs of a problem, with the comb and/or wattles having black edges or marks as the frost kills off cells and, in more extreme cases, parts of the comb and wattles may even be missing. This will undoubtedly be very painful for a bird, but in the case of a valuable show bird it will certainly prevent it from winning prizes and could also reduce the bird's value dramatically.

> *Coating the wattles and comb generously with Vaseline will provide considerable protection from the weather.*

Simply coating the wattles and comb generously with Vaseline first thing in the morning, especially when there is a heavy frost, will provide considerable protection from the weather. Rub the Vaseline gently all over the comb and wattles, giving them quite a thick coating. Applying Vaseline will cause no discomfort whatsoever to the birds, but it will certainly help to prevent or at least reduce the effects of frostbite. This is rarely fatal for a bird but it must be very painful and uncomfortable for them.

A Brief Description of the Comb

The Latin or scientific description of the chicken is *Gallus Domesticus*, the word *Gallus* meaning comb. A chicken's actual comb is the fleshy red section that sits on the top of the bird's head. It is, in most cases, larger on the male than the female and there are several different types of comb. These vary considerably, depending on the individual breed of chicken concerned.

The comb certainly helps to distinguish and identify different breeds. A good example is the Silkie which carries a 'Cushion comb' that is unique to the breed. Many other breeds such as the Leghorn carry a single large comb, with the male showing the comb standing straight, whereas the female's lies over to one side – an acceptable trait in the breed, even in the show pen. The Rhode Island Red can sport either a large single comb or a rose comb, with the single comb being the most common and recognisable in this very well-known breed.

The single comb.

What Purpose Does the Comb Serve?

The comb certainly helps a bird to keep cool in hot weather. Chickens do not sweat, but their blood is cooled down on hot days as it flows through both the comb and the wattles, reducing the temperature of the bird as the blood runs throughout the body. It is also believed that a large comb attracts the females, as chickens are attracted to the colour red. A bird's comb is certainly at its reddest and brightest when birds are at their most fertile, and this applies to the female too.

The Single Comb

A single comb is by far the most common in chickens. This type of comb is very much the typical one usually represented in pictures and on poultry related ornaments. It is a moderately thin, fleshy comb with a smooth texture which sits firmly on top of the head from the beak to the back of the skull. It normally has five or six serrations and the

The rose comb.

The walnut comb.

The pea comb.

middle points are usually higher. The male comb almost always tends to be larger than the female and this type of comb is mostly straight, although in some breeds the female comb may droop over. Dependent on the breed standard, this can be an acceptable variation.

The Rose Comb

This is a solid, broad and low comb which is almost flat on top. It tapers to the rear in a small spike and some breeds such as the Hamburg may have this spike turning upwards. Typically, as with the Wyandotte, it follows the contours of the head and lies flat, although the specific shape can vary according to the individual breed. It can also come with a long leader.

The Pea Comb

This is a medium length low comb and the top is normally marked with three low length wide ridges. The centre ridge is usually slightly higher, and they have small rounded serrations. This type of comb is found on breeds such as the Brahma, Sumatra and Cornish.

The Walnut Comb

Shaped like the nut from which it takes its name,

the walnut comb can come in a full 'walnut' shape, but can also have the appearance of being just half a walnut. The Malay is possibly the best-known breed sporting this type of comb.

The Horn Comb

This type of comb is limited to only a few breeds and, as the description implies, has the appearance of horns. Breeds such as the Crevecoeur, La Fleche, Houdan and Sultan can all show a variation of this type of comb.

The cushion comb.

Coryza.

The Cushion Comb

The appearance of this type of comb is also very much as the name implies, and is quite well known as one of most outstanding features of the male Silkie chicken. The comb can vary considerably in size, but can be quite large and is also a very attractive mulberry colour.

Eye Problems

A chicken's eyes can be affected by a number of different problems, most of which are related to a variety of respiratory problems including colds, roup, vitamin deficiency, coryza, fowl pox, conjunctivitis and dusty litter.

Dusty Litter

This problem originates in the bedding area and is easy to avoid through good and proper management and a little common sense. Use only dust-extracted shavings – never straw, hay or sawdust, and replace it regularly.

Coryza

This is a respiratory condition that is more or less a cold. The symptoms are a watery discharge from the eyes and beak. *Coryza* is a bacterial infection and as such is very infectious. In truth many of these types of infection can be confused as the symptoms are very similar. One major cause of respiratory infection among chickens can be high ammonia levels in the coop which can cause breathing difficulties and even blindness in extreme cases. The problem can be treated with antibiotics.

Sinusitis

If your birds are suffering from the symptoms of coryza, they can be compounded with a swelling and inflammation of the sinuses under the eyes – this is a far more serious complaint altogether. The symptoms are a watery discharge from the corner of the eye and mucus from the beak. The cause is respiratory and an accurate diagnosis will need to be made.

Gently cleaning the eye.

Sinusitis.

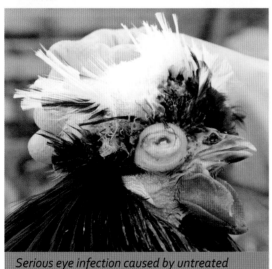
Serious eye infection caused by untreated crest mite.

Swelling of the Head (often Avian Rhinotracheitis)

If this occurs then several birds may be affected. It is normally a sign of avian *rhinotracheitis* and any affected birds will look very ill. You will most likely encounter a high rate of mortality. Avian *rhinotracheitis* is now well established in many chicken flocks and contributes to many respiratory outbreaks. To confirm an outbreak of avian *rhinotracheitis* you will need to have blood tests done. There is a vaccination but it is not always satisfactory, especially when there is a variation in the ages of the birds.

Crest Mite

High maintenance birds such as the Poland are susceptible to crest mite. Keep the eyes clear and clean and wash the crest feathers on a regular basis to avoid black crest mite. These mites are very visible so check routinely for them, and the regular use of an anti-mite spray or a good louse powder should help to avoid problems.

Chapter Nine

Problems with the Legs and Feet

Scaly Leg Mite

This used to be called foot mange or scabies and it is a serious problem for *all* poultry, including pheasants and turkeys. Waterfowl, however, rarely seem to suffer from it. The name more or less explains the nature of the complaint – the appearance of raised and rough scales which worsen as the problem grows. The cause is actually a mite which burrows under the scales to lay its eggs, causing the scales to rise. As the young hatch this causes them to be raised even more. These attacks tend to take place from the top of the toes up to the leg. If untreated the scales will eventually fall off, leaving the legs bare. The problem must be treated well before this stage is reached. In nearly all cases both legs will be affected and, although not as serious as some other mites, scaly leg mites can and do cripple birds, in turn creating ever more problems including infection, which can prove to be very serious.

The problem of scaly leg mite is usually transmitted through dirty litter and these mite can live away from birds for quite some time. Before you transfer new stock into any shed which has previously housed birds with scaly leg mite, a thorough clean and disinfecting is essential. Isolate any birds suffering from the problem as it spreads rapidly given the chance.

Prevention is straight forward enough – check your birds' legs regularly for loose or lifting scales and, under no circumstances, buy in any birds showing signs; you will simply be buying yourself a lot of trouble.

Keeping your birds in a clean environment with regular bedding changes should keep the problem at bay, and is simply common sense and good management in any case.

A very bad example of scaly leg.

Healthy feet and legs. There should be no signs of swelling, lumps or bumps.

Old fashioned treatments involved substances being painted onto the legs, but most of them are no longer available, although painting the legs with surgical spirit or *duramitex* will work wonders. Once painted and dry, cover the entire leg and foot with Vaseline which will suffocate any remaining mites that the painting has failed to kill. It will also help with the healing process of the scales. *Johnson's* make a special scaly leg dropper available on prescription which works through the bird's blood system. Although inexpensive it is only available in a very small bottle, which means if you have a large number of birds then painting is probably the more practical alternative. Whatever solution you choose, it is a problem which needs prompt action to prevent it spreading.

Marek's Disease

This is a disease that affects a bird's mobility. It is caused by the herpes virus and, once established, is difficult to eradicate. Affected birds show a variety of symptoms including twisted necks, walking round in circles and stargazing, but the most common sign is paralysis which causes the birds legs to splay out, eventually resulting in a total loss of mobility. The mortality rate for affected birds is 100% and the disease may affect up to 50% of a flock. The appearance of the problem can start with chicks as young as 3 weeks old, but is more common in birds of around 12 to 30 weeks of age. Deaths will usually start at 8 to 10 weeks and will carry on until the birds reach 20 to 25 weeks of age.

A vaccination against *Marek's* disease is available and if there are *any* signs of the disease or likelihood of it occurring, vaccination is essential to protect the other birds in the flock, but needs to take place as the birds are hatched.

Disease of the Hip

This problem is more common in birds reared intensively for meat where rapid growth is required, but it does affect other birds too. In a fashion not dissimilar to people, it involves the degeneration and infection of the hip joints. The

Problems with the Legs and Feet

Crooked toes in an adult bird.

Rickets

Not dissimilar to the problems seen in children many years ago, this term is used loosely to describe various types of skeletal problems, and usually refers to the incorrect calcification of the bones, especially in developing chicks between 10 days and 6 weeks of age. The birds will show signs of paralysis, usually resulting in mortality. Always ensure that the diet of *any* young chicks immediately after hatching includes calcium to help prevent the problem. Most bought feeds suitable for chicks of this age will be manufactured to include the appropriate levels of calcium.

Paralysis

This is more usually a symptom rather than an ailment, and can be the result of many different diseases and conditions found in chickens. These include Marek's disease, brittle bone, rickets, vitamin E deficiency and kinky back.

Burnt Hocks

A condition common in broiler chickens, this is caused by the legs continually coming into contact with litter as the birds lie down. The heat and the ammonia from the often soiled litter actually burn the legs and the infection then spreads into the hocks, eventually causing lameness.

signs are a reluctance to walk due to the pain of doing so. There is really no practical cure, although there is an ongoing investigation into the problem. Mortality, mostly due to an inability to function properly, is almost 100% over a period of time.

Deformed Toes

Chicks can sometimes hatch with deformed toes, and this can be due to a genetic problem passed on through adult stock. It can also be caused by incorrect temperature settings during incubation. Ultimately it may make proper perching impossible. Where perching is possible, care must be taken at a later stage as incorrect perching will only exacerbate the problem. Make sure perches are rounded along the upper edges and not set too high above the ground as bad landings can cause problems too (see 'Bumblefoot' below). Deformed toes are more common in meat birds and laying birds reared in intensive units. Birds with deformed toes can often lead full and complete lives.

Bumblefoot

This is a swelling on or under the foot and is generally caused by a *staphylococcal* infection. The most common symptom is a swelling under the foot with a visible central core. Perching too high is believed to be one of the main causes as heavier birds can puncture the foot pad when jumping down onto uneven or rough ground, leading to the infection. Very rough perches can also create the same problem, so whenever you are replacing perches, sand them down and round off any sharp edges.

Chapter Ten

Hens with Special Needs

The most obvious birds with special needs are the now familiar ex-battery birds, which may never even have seen the outdoors prior to their retirement from the commercial world. I have tried here to deal with the question of combining different birds, dealing with particularly nervous birds and keeping fancy fowl, a number of which are rather high maintenance in terms of the work their unusual plumage creates for the keeper. In many respects *all* chickens have their own special needs, in the sense that they will add considerably to the duties of any new chicken keeper, and the following examples will require just that little bit extra TLC, but the returns should be well worth it as your ex-battery birds enjoy their very first dust bath, or your prize Poland takes first prize at the local poultry event.

Care of Ex-battery or Barn-reared Birds

When taking on this type of chicken there are certain considerations that you *must* take into account – these birds have known nothing other than the inside of an intensive production unit for the whole of their lives. Usually they have never even seen the outdoors or natural sunlight, and have only ever been fed on a specialist feed designed to maintain a high level of egg production. However, chickens do respond to change and with patience you should see a dramatic improvement over a month or two.

Points to Consider

Birds can easily be stressed by such a complete change in their environment. After being removed from the cages and placed in a free range environment or a run, they must suddenly feel as though they have been transported to a different planet. They will require a period of quiet and time to settle in and explore their new home at their own speed if serious stress levels are to be avoided. Try to keep your distance and leave it to the birds to approach you as they eventually begin to associate you with the arrival of food. This relaxed transition to their new environment will make it much more manageable for them, and should in most cases enable them to enjoy a long and happy retirement.

The Healthy Hens Handbook

Feeding

A sudden change in feed can also result in birds throwing pellets out of the feeder – this may be the result of them not actually realising that it is in fact feed. They will, however, adapt very quickly and become used to the new feed.

> **"** *Never fear... I cannot recall a chicken that could resist anything edible for more than a short while!* **"**

There are feeds available which are designed specifically for ex-battery hens. Usually they are in the form of a crumb feed containing extra protein and other minerals, which are very important in helping these hens return to a healthy condition. In truth though, any standard layers' pellets from a reputable manufacturer together with extra vitamin supplements, grit and a constant supply of fresh water should be sufficient to bring them back into peak condition over a short period of time

When the birds arrive it is highly likely they will have a very poor and sad appearance with a lack of feathers, large patches of bare skin, and they may be underweight and unsteady on their legs due to their earlier confinement. Although battery cages in the traditional sense were outlawed from the beginning of 2012, the replacements, although a huge improvement on the earlier cages and with considerably more room to move, are still just a more humane variation of the concept, with birds still kept indoors and confined, but in greater spaces and together with other birds rather than separated by wire mesh. The birds will regain their health and condition, and the feathers will return given time and the correct diet, but it may take some time for them to regain the normal appearance of the standard brown hen with which we are all familiar.

Ex-battery chickens with feathers in a poor state.

Moulting

Although newly acquired ex-battery hens will more than likely be in poor condition as regards plumage when you receive them, they will more than likely begin to moult early on. This will prevent them from laying for a short period as their energy is diverted into acquiring new feathers, but even though they may not be laying, keep them on a ration of layers' pellets as they will need all the ingredients to regrow their plumage.

Vaccinations

Commercial battery chickens are normally vaccinated, and sometimes overly so as a compensation for their unnatural environment, which can cause problems if you introduce them

Flo (Florence), an ex-battery chicken 3 months on from being rescued.

directly into an existing flock, especially if the existing birds have not been vaccinated. There is always a chance that the vaccinated birds might be carriers of the various diseases for which they have been vaccinated. Consequently, keep them in isolation before adding them to an existing flock until you are completely satisfied that they are clear of disease and have replaced most of their missing feathers. If they are introduced prior to having restored their plumage they may, in some cases, be bullied by your existing birds, and this can become very serious and occasionally fatal if not kept under control.

Ex-battery hens are usually 18 months old when they are replaced. They will have been through an extremely extensive egg laying period during this time, and although they may no longer be up to full industry-level performance, they will still be more than capable of supplying you with eggs on a regular basis.

Perches/Nest Boxes

Barn hens will at least have some idea when it comes to using nest boxes and perches, but ex-battery hens will have absolutely no idea what they are for. To get them used to perching you will have to *place them* on the perches as they become more passive in the evening when it goes dark, and repeat this several times until they get the idea that this is what they should be doing as birds, and for their own good – roosting clear of soiled or moist bedding will help prevent mite and other insect infestation and keep the birds in considerably better health than if sleeping directly on bedding. Putting perches and nest boxes quite low will help initially until they eventually become accustomed to using them as returning to the coop each evening becomes second nature. As with most things, your patience as a keeper will win out in the end.

A very young chick with splayed legs, possibly caused by an overly smooth floor in the brooder, which made getting a grip impossible when taking those all-important early steps.

Poorly Birds

Any birds showing signs of illness will need immediate treatment, and wherever possible should be separated from other birds, even at a very early age in the brooder as with the chick in the photograph above. It is ideal if you can keep a small area solely for the purpose of housing birds that are, or become, poorly. By keeping them separate you can often prevent illness or disease from spreading, and confinement is certainly the safest and easiest way of doing this.

Often poorly hens are *not* carrying an infectious disease, but if birds are in any way poorly they may suddenly become victims of bullying by healthy members of the flock. By separating unhealthy birds from the flock it will prevent them from becoming targets for healthy birds to pick on and prevent bullying, which can become a major problem if left to continue unchecked, especially during the longer periods of overnight confinement in the coop in winter.

Nervous Hens

Quite frankly most breeds of poultry are nervous... some could probably be described as downright cowardly, with the exception of certain roosters with attitude, in which case everything around becomes a potential target for attack, and usually even more so during the breeding season.

Extremely nervous birds do need to be treated with appropriate care as their stress factor is undoubtedly the main single challenge they need to deal with.

Some birds, however, are exceptionally nervous and may have been victims at some point in their

Chickens are social animals who usually sort out their own hierarchy without any problems.

lives. It is extremely unlikely that you will be able do anything for them, other than trying to make their lives as simple and unstressed as possible, which usually means leaving them to get on with things, with you as the keeper simply providing food, drink and ocasional treats or supplements.

If you need to catch such birds, wait until dusk or even later to do it whilst they are roosting, as this reduces the chances of having to chase them around the pen. If ever you need to examine them during the day and in good light, use a net to prevent the trauma of a chase – the bird will not be happy, but the stress will at least be brief and short-lived.

Most birds, if treated with care, will eventually settle down, and in most cases become quite tame. This can take a considerable period of time and patience on your part, but if you avoid rushing into pens, refrain from wearing very bright clothing (especially red, as this seems to excite certain types of bird), move slowly, allowing birds to move out of your way at their own pace, and make feed times a pleasure (undeniably their favourite form of human interaction), they will very soon lose much of their fear as they become used to you entering their world. Again, patience will achieve the best results.

Hens that Have Been Bullied

Birds that have been bullied will need to be separated and kept calm. Bullying causes immense stress, and stress itself can be a killer. Even in an all-female pen there may be times when a bird is, for one reason or another, just not accepted by the other birds, and this can result in that bird becoming a complete outcast and under constant threat. Such a bird will hide and cower in a corner, or refuse to leave the coop, but it should be difficult for an observant keeper not to notice that something is very wrong. If this happens, separate the bird and keep it on its own for reasons of safety. Try, if at all possible, to relocate any such birds, unless you have another pen where they might live happily and be accepted by your other birds.

A crest showing signs of damage through pecking and regrowth of new feathers.

Birds of a similar size will usually get on well.

Bird Socialisation

Chickens are, for the most part, quite sociable, but some breeds seem to find it difficult to live together in harmony. Certain breeds, especially game birds, will fight, and this applies to both males and females.

Under most circumstances, hens of a similar size and breed will live together reasonably well, at least after the initial introduction, when there will almost certainly be a number of arguments as to who is boss (hence the term 'ruling the roost'), but once a pecking order has been established, birds will get along without any real further problems. There is no hard and fast rule as to how to best introduce new birds, but doing so at night time into a dark coop will help to minimize any initial disturbance, and if you are looking to introduce a significant number of birds, allow them to get close but separated by chicken wire so that they can get used to each other before the proper introduction takes place.

It is a good idea to try and keep all the birds in your flock roughly the same size, and keep fancy and colourful breeds separate from standard laying hybrid birds, as they can prove to be a target for the commercial breeds.

Keeping game birds together with soft feathered birds is definitely not a good idea as the game birds will, without doubt, cause problems for any less aggressive breeds. If you are looking to mix more traditional breeds in a flock together with hybrids then doing it with very young birds will be more successful than with birds at point of lay.

A White Crested Black Poland cockerel.

Other Special Needs

Some birds, often referred to as fancy breeds, also require special care due to their unusual plumage. This is very much the case with crested Polands and Houdans and, to a lesser extent, Silkies, with a fine covering of feathers that was originally likened to the fur on a cat. There are also breeds with feathered feet and legs, such as Brahmas, Cochins and Langshans which have their own unique requirements.

Crested varieties should be kept separate from standard breeds, and preferably under cover. They are almost always kept as exhibition birds and need considerably more attention than any ordinary chickens due to their impressive crests, which, while they are undoubtedly the birds' main attraction, are also their main weakness and the reason why they are often described as 'high maintenance.' The crests are prone to mite infestation, and as a consequence of the crested covering they can also suffer from eye problems too. This problem is further compounded by the fact that many birds today have been bred incorrectly, making the above problems even worse in such birds. Polands also have restricted vision, making them even more vulnerable to attack if kept together with other types of bird.

A bad eye infection caused by neglect of the crest above the eye.

Keeping the crest clean and mite free is of the utmost importance. Shampooing birds with a dog or cat flea shampoo works well, with the bird wrapped in a towel with the head well forward, which helps to make it feel safe and secure and prevents any struggling. Gently wet the crest, shampoo carefully and rinse when any mites have been removed. The birds can then be left to dry naturally on warm days, or using a hair dryer on less warm days, but keep wet birds away from dry birds. I am often asked in disbelief why I wash a chicken, and my usual answer is, "If they become soiled and dirty, then why not?" We have birds who really enjoy being washed and others who are less happy about it.

We use Frontline on the crest as a treatment to keep mite and other insects at bay – it works wonders and lasts for up to six months after each application. It is not a licensed product for poultry use, but is recommended by vets in the UK. Needless to say, with any kind of spray or aerosol, do not spray anywhere near the eyes, mouth and nose, which should be simple common sense.

With certain crested birds the front vision may be hampered. You can either trim the crest carefully using a sharp pair of scissors, or alternatively, tape it up using automotive masking tape, which can be removed with no discomfort or damage to a bird. If cutting you must be careful if a bird becomes spooked and begins to struggle, especially if cutting close to the eyes, and if using tape, mite will almost certainly be attracted to a taped-up crest, so remove the tape regularly to check the condition.

A final problem with crested birds is encountered when they try to feed and drink; the crest puts them at an immediate disadvantage, and it is not advisable to use any kind of open or wide-rimmed drinker, as the crest will rapidly become wet and soiled and even more attractive to insect infestation, with even greater risk of eye problems and infection. Narrow-lipped drinkers are an essential requirement, and pellets accompanied by occasional corn are the best feeding options. Any food which becomes either powdery or dusty, especially when the crest is wet, will most likely create further problems for both the eyes and the plumage.

The requirements for birds with feathered legs and feet are considerably less than for crested birds, with mud being the most difficult potential problem. In all other respects they are very much standard pure breed birds, capable of living together with other birds and spending much of the time outside. The Brahma, often referred to as a gentle giant, is a most impressive bird, and a firm showing favourite, but with considerably fewer drawbacks than their crested counterparts.

White Crested Mottled Poland

Chapter Eleven

From Backyard to Show Pen

Keeping chickens for eggs and as family pets in the back garden as a hobby is of course great fun; you get a productive pet that provides you with a supply of fresh eggs. But why not add to that pleasure and expand the hobby to include exhibiting your birds at a local poultry show, the ideal first step into the more competitive world of showing, which has increased dramatically in popularity over the last few years. Take my word for it – once you have made the effort and become involved in this fascinating and completely different part of the poultry hobby, you will find that there are many new friends to be made and a great social side to the many different events that take place all over the country.

To get a first idea of what is actually involved it is always a good idea to go to one of your local agricultural shows – there will be many within a short car ride of you every summer – and visit the poultry tent. This will give you a good idea as to how shows are conducted, and there will be plenty of people there keen to answer any questions and to guide you towards your first attempt at exhibiting your birds. Although it may be a competitive aspect of the poultry world, the general view is pretty straight forward – the more, the merrier – and you will be warmly welcomed.

There are of course a few points which you must take into account before you even consider entering your first show, mainly you must be fully aware of the rules and regulations which are in place at each individual venue. These will have been developed over many years and to question them as the 'new kid on the block' would be unwise. They are there for a reason, often the welfare of birds, and as such, make sure you comply with them and respect the processes involved.

The most important of all these rules is that birds which are entered and put on show must all be 'pure bred'.

Modern Jungle Fowl.

The most important of all the rules is that birds entered and put on show *must* be 'pure bred', meaning that they must be a recognised breed kept as pure blooded as possible. Any bird entered must also represent the correct standard as laid down by the Poultry Club of Great Britain in conjunction with the standards set by the individual breed clubs, who effectively act as guardians of the individual breeds they represent.

Virtually all organised poultry shows are covered by these rules and if you are not quite sure about your own birds you can check them by contacting the relevant breed club (just type the breed name into your Internet search engine) or the Poultry Club of Great Britain, as both of these organisations will be able to supply you with the correct standard a

bird needs to fulfil. Most breed websites include details of the standard, so checking is a simple matter. Reading about the subject is also a good idea as you can check your own birds as you read about them. There are certainly many books on the market with excellent pictures from which you can get a comparison of just how your bird should look. The *British Breed Standards* book is updated regularly to provide the latest details of new birds accepted into the register and amendments to existing standards or new requirements.

There are a small number of exceptions to these rules, and some smaller country shows do include a section for 'pet birds', and also some junior sections which accept entries just for pleasure. As times and habits change, so eventually do rules,

Frizzled feathers will need extra care.

Feathered legs on Brahmas take some looking after.

but it's a slow process and the primary purpose of exhibiting remains to preserve stock which the Rare Breed Survival Trust describes as 'under threat', so bloodlines and breeds are and will always remain important in the show circuit.

> *These less formal events do, however, provide fun for many people who can show even their domestic egg laying birds.*

Even though your birds may be hybrids and classed as pet birds, they will still need to be washed and prepared in order to be allowed into the show pens – even in these less formal events standards remain high and dirty birds are *not* acceptable, so even though they may not come under show rules as regards judging, they still have to be presentable and look their very best.

The number and range of breeds which do qualify for exhibitiing is considerable, and most of these variations can be found on the Poultry Club of Great Britain website. There are now so many that it is not possible or practical to list them all here, but the most popular ones include the Silkie, Rhode Island Red, Pekin, Orpington, Leghorn, Japanese, Austrolorp, Old English Game and Maran. The list goes on, and all of the birds included on it have their own individual standard of perfection, and should be bred and reared to reflect that standard.

The different standard for each breed will include feather colour and quality, eye and beak colour, general markings and the appearance of the head and body. Equally important though is the general condition of the birds which need to look fit and healthy and excellent examples of the breed they are representing. Each breed standard also includes a comprehensive list of more common defects which will disqualify a bird from competing, so make yourself familiar with these before selecting a bird to show. There must also be no signs of illness or infestation by insects on your chosen bird (lice and mite on a bird will quite rightly mean immediate disqualification). The following are the main points you will need to consider before deciding to enter any birds into competition.

The crest must be washed to rid it of mite and prepare it for the show.

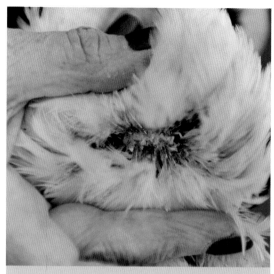

Evidence of crest mite.

Entering a Bird

This is probably the easiest part. Find someone who shows chickens (you may even know someone who does, but just not be aware of it), or contact a local poultry club to find out local show dates and information on times and other essential details. If this proves difficult then phone or email the Poultry Club of Great Britain which should be able to help. Once you have located one or more events, the show schedules will be provided and posted to you by a show secretary. These show schedules will usually contain sections in the form that will require you to enrol for membership of the show in question, and this will entitle you to a discount on your entry fees and allow you to win the awards presented at the show – in most cases a non-member *can* win, but *cannot* collect prizes.

You will have to fill in and answer a number of questions on an entry form requiring details of the birds and their sex. Descriptions of the classes available to enter can vary slightly from show to show, but all will have a listing of individual breeds. Occasionally in smaller shows some breeds have to be included together in the same classes simply due to the size of the event, and in this case you will have to find out the class into which you should enter your birds. Every breed comes under the broad classification of Soft Feather Heavy, Soft Feather Light, Hard Feather, Rare Breed plus True Bantam (see Chapter 3, Know Your Chickens, and the clasifications on pages 25-29). The most popular at events are the soft feather breeds which come in both Bantam and Large and include familiar breeds such as the Rhode Island Red, Brahma, Cochin, Leghorn, Silkie, Poland, Sussex and many more.

Once you have entered your schedule, make sure to include payment for pens at the show. Costs will vary from show to show but payment details will be included in the individual schedules. Always post your entry in good time; show secretaries will always have a closing date on the schedule to make sure they have sufficient time to organise everything for the show. Aim to send in your entry or entries some 3 to 4 weeks before the actual event as this will definitely help the organisers to sort everything out in good time.

A real show stopper!

Selecting Your Show Birds

Picking your ideal show birds is one of the most important parts of the process, and one of the most difficult too. The wrong choice of bird may be the difference between winning and losing (although there really are no losers). Any bird or birds you may be considering showing should be as close to the standard as possible. They will need to look and walk properly, their feathers must be completely intact with none broken or missing; in fact any faults in the plumage will not win prizes. Check the weight of your bird too to make sure it is as suggested in the breed standard, and make sure they look both fit and healthy with bright eyes, an alert disposition and perky appearance.

Once you have selected your birds, inspect them one at a time, checking closely for any defects such as missing toe nails, a twisted breast bone, knock knees, lice or mite and crossed beaks, plus take a very close look now at the condition of the plumage.

Once you have satisfied yourself that all these points are in order, make sure that the legs, beak, eyes and plumage are within the colour descriptions in the breed standards.

Once you have satisfied all the visual requirements for the standard, it will be down to your own judgement to pick the best birds to show. If you have observed and come to know your birds as recommended in earlier chapters, this should now be a reasonably straight forward decision.

Pen Training

Pen training will probably be the first step in your show preparation and involves training your birds in a pen similar to those used at shows. Let them use smaller drinkers too such as those that will be available at the event on the day. This is because your birds will need to be calm and relaxed when contained in pens considerably smaller and different to those they are probably used to. This can take a couple of weeks and the training should include handling your birds regularly so that when they are handled for judging they will readily allow the judge to do so. Done well, this preparation will help your bird to stand out from the crowd.

To put a bird in a pen with no advance training can be very stressful due to the strange environment.

Always be gentle with your bird so that it does not become panicked, and make sure it is comfortable and settled. Most birds will adapt very quickly to new circumstances, but some never take to show pens and will therefore always be unsuitable for exhibiting. If you are unfortunate enough to own one of these birds, use it for breeding by all means, but leave it out of the show pens.

The Healthy Hens Handbook

Transporting Birds to a Show

Attending most poultry shows will mean an early start. Birds must be penned and ready for the judges reasonably early in the morning, usually by 9 or 9.30am. Check your entry form for any variation to this, but you will need to be there at least an hour before to prepare and get the birds penned. Penning slips together with your cage numbers are sometimes sent by post or can be collected on the day when they are normally laid out on a table for you to pick up. They will include all the pen numbers you have been allocated, and these numbers should match the numbers on your slip. As a final check, make sure your birds are in the correct pens, but if you are not completely sure then ask an official for help.

Before you leave home you will need a suitable box with plenty of ventilation. You can still use a cardboard box but the rules regarding carry boxes are changing and eventually we will all have to use a properly constructed poultry carrying box. Whichever type you use, make sure there are plenty of shavings in the bottom as this will help to keep the birds clean during the journey. Also do not put water inside the carry box whilst in transit as it will spill. Instead stop regularly to make sure your birds drink frequently. Make sure they are comfortable too and have enough room to be able to move without breaking any feathers whilst inside the box. Many exhibitors transport their show birds in a narrow box with plenty of height and air which stops them turning inside the box and therefore reduces feather breakage.

Once in transit the birds will settle down, and in most cases will sleep. This is why well ventilated but darker carry boxes are usually better. When transporting birds I always try to keep them inside the car or van as this gives them air and prevents them from becoming overheated and stressed, especially in summer.

The most time consuming part of showing is preparing your birds for judging and viewing by the general public. You can't hope to simply pull a bird straight out of a pen or field and put it into a show pen. Any birds which are dirty and not prepared are not acceptable and will usually be disqualified. During their daily routine birds dig, enjoy dust baths and show a real fascination for the dirtiest areas such as a fresh compost heap. They become dirty very quickly, especially during damp or wet weather, which is unfortunately often the summer show season norm.

Your selected showing birds should be brought inside at least a week before a show, which will give you sufficient time to wash and dry them before the event.

Washing and Preparation

You do need to wash and prepare your birds for a show. It is of the utmost importance that they are in a clean and healthy condition, so a full body wash is recommended to make sure they are both really clean and lice free. Insects can always be seen more easily when a bird is wet, so use this opportunity to check them thoroughly for lice and mite. An insect shampoo such as those used on cats and dogs will be ideal as they are safe to use and help to control both insects and their eggs. They are readily available and reasonably inexpensive from pet shops.

It is a good idea to use a bowl or a sink to wash a bird, with the bird standing in the water. A spray tap will be ideal for wetting and rinsing, but if this is not available then have a second bowl ready containing clean warm water for rinsing. Handle the bird gently, taking care not to submerge it completely, and always take into consideration the levels of stress this may cause the bird. If there are any signs of stress such as gasping or beak opening then stop and allow a little time for recovery before continuing.

Once washed it is easiest to wrap a bird in a towel which will help remove a lot of the water. You can then use a hair dryer on a low warm setting to help speed up the drying process, or if the weather is nice and warm they could dry naturally on their own, although away from possible dust baths or compost heaps. I always dry birds at least a little to make sure they do not become chilled, and I prefer presonally not to put them outside as they can chill very easily, especially in the British climate.

Once a bird is dry, settled and comfortable you will need to check once more for any insects. This is also a good time to spray the birds with a good recognised anti-mite spray, of which there are several available, although they are not all licensed for chickens. Ask your supplier and they will advise you on the best product for your needs. You can use a good quality organic powder which can be anti-lice and anti-mite. To apply it, hold the bird securely and powder under the wings and around the vent area, making sure the powder goes well into the feathers and down to the skin in much the same way we might apply talcum powder to ourselves.

A washed bird will need at least a few days to replace lost oil from the feathers which may have been removed during washing; this is, however, a normal and natural process and does no harm to a bird. I also prefer to keep them in show cages at this stage just prior to the event to make sure there are no unnoticed cases of feather pecking – two birds confined in a small area quickly become bored, which can create problems such as aggression.

Next in the process is a manicure as the beaks and nails need to be clean and, if necessary, cut and trimmed slightly. This is in many ways very similar to a normal manicure, but with the odd subtle difference. Always trim both the beak and nails very, very carefully, and do not over trim as this will cause bleeding. Then, once the nails are

Rinsing the crest.

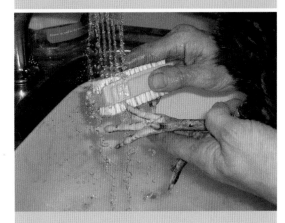
Scrubbing feet clean.

Applying louse and mite powder.

Welsummer hen.

trimmed, finish off with a nail file to shape and smooth them.

After the manicure it is time to concentrate on the legs – all poultry have scales on their legs and this is a place where birds get particularly dirty, so use an old tooth brush together with some good soap and clean the scales really well. The legs will soon look bright and clean, then do just the same to the toes and under the feet as all these places are checked by the judge on show day.

Finally, make sure the nose, eyes, face, comb and wattles are all bright and clean. Sponge them gently with a soft cloth and warm soapy water. This should give the required appearance for the event.

Applying a final treatment to the comb.

> *You can also add a little baby oil or comb and wattle treatment on a cotton wool bud to make the face and wattles look extra red and shiny, but I prefer to do this on the day of the event, just before penning.*

Final Preparations at the Show

When you arrive at the show and locate your pen, make sure there are enough shavings on the floor; this is important as it will keep birds cleaner for the judging. Carefully remove the bird from your carry box, checking the legs, feet and feathers to make sure they have not become soiled during the journey. This is when a small but essential kit box containing a damp cloth, a face treatment, a silk cloth, and in some cases even a battery-powered hair dryer, comes in handy. Just check your birds and touch up any parts that require it before placing them in the show pen. Comb and wattle treatment can be applied at this time, and there

are specially made treatments on the market, but a cotton wool bud and some baby oil can work wonders. Don't apply too much though as it can appear a little sticky if you overdo it.

Just before the judging it is better if feed and water is removed from the show pen. It can soon become untidy as feed and water are inevitably splashed around in a small space, soiling the birds at the critical moment just before the judge casts his eye over them. The birds will have been fed and watered both before and during the journey, so there is no reason to worry too much about them during the relatively short period of judging. Then, when judging is complete, they can be fed and watered as normal.

When you are eventually happy that you have done everything to your satisfaction, walk away and have a coffee while you await the results. Under no circumstances should you bother the judge while he is going about his task; this would be considered very unprofessional. If you have

Final preparations for the show... Bath Time!

any questions wait until he has finished and then ask whatever you need to know. Always ask it in a proper manner and do not challenge the judge's decision, although you could ask why your bird did not win, if that is the case, and he or she will usually be keen to help you learn for next time. Remember though that each and every judge will most likely have a different opinion, so it comes down to an individual opinion on that particular day, but the judge will usually be an experienced poultry expert, so use the opportunity to ask and learn from them.

Caring for Birds during and after Judging

Whilst the judging is in process you should not approach or touch your birds. Indeed, at many shows the public and exhibitors are not allowed in the show area during judging. This helps prevent cheating, but when the judge has completed your section and the prize cards are on the cages you can do whatever is needed to feed, water and care for your birds. Some exhibitors put in a cut apple for the birds to peck at and this helps to keep them occupied. Drinkers, if in place, need to be securely fastened to prevent spillages as if your birds become soiled or dirty at this event, they may not recover for the next one you have entered. Just keep a regular check on their welfare and make sure they are not handled by anyone without your permission, other than the judge. The only reason for the removal of a bird should be to either to show you any faults, to give you help for future showing or to take photographs. I often see people taking out a bird for no obvious reason, and all this does is to put it under unnecessary stress and increases the chances of spreading diseases.

Returning Home and Quarantining Birds to Prevent Disease

At the end of the show the organiser will announce the closing of the event and give permission for everyone to box their birds.

Do not remove any of your birds before this announcement is made; it is done this way for everyone's security and to make sure that no birds go missing.

Once the birds are packed away and everyone is satisfied that they have all their livestock, the exhibitors will be allowed to depart and consider the day's events. Boxing and travelling are just the same as in the morning, only in reverse. The main difference should be that when you arrive home you have a place set aside which is separate from your other birds – this is referred to as quarantine, and it is for your own good as showing birds alongside other birds, often from all over the country, can be a risk as regards the spread of diseases. All you need is a simple separate area where you can put your show stock for up to two weeks, by which time any infections will have been noticed. Then you can reintroduce them back into the flock.

Do not by any means let this put you off showing as in all the years we have exhibited poultry we have never had a serious problem. We will, however, continue to take these same precautions which should also apply whenever you buy in new stock and introduce them to your own. Bio-security is very important in today's world for both the safety of our birds *and* our own safety.

Chapter Twelve

Breeding a Healthy Hen

Incubation

What Can Go Wrong?

There are many different reasons why things might go wrong when trying to hatch chicks using artificial incubation, most of which I will try and cover in the following chapter. It is always easy to blame the machine/incubator but they will only operate if they are positioned correctly, set to the recommended settings and cleaned and operated in the proper manner. What follows should enable you to do this with confidence.

Incubation is the method used to hatch eggs artificially. For many beginners the idea might be a little daunting, but if you take your time and research the subject it can be a very rewarding and exciting part of chicken keeping. One of the main problems for the beginner is understanding and accepting what may have gone wrong when there are failures. Everyone who uses an incubator is going to have both successes and failures — even if you are an expert the results can vary quite

dramatically. It's just a question of making sure the successes are far greater than the failures and recording how you did it each time so you can learn from any earlier mistakes. The way to do this is to try and understand the reasons for those failures so you can prevent them from happening again.

Collecting Eggs for Incubation

If you are using your own eggs then before you even consider putting them into an incubator you will need to be sure that the cockerel in question is performing properly. The birds all need to be healthy, and you need to have everything ready to be able to collect the eggs ready for putting them into the incubator.

If you watch the birds you will see the cockerel 'treading', or mating. He will climb onto the female's back and mating then takes place. If the male is not interested or shows no signs of interest, then fertility is highly unlikely and setting eggs will probably be a futile excercise. The fertility of the birds is something we cannot judge until the eggs are set, and when candled show signs

Washing an egg before placing it in the incubator.

of development; this will serve as definite proof that they are fertile. Provided that the birds are looking healthy and alert and active with bright red combs, there is a very good chance of them providing good results.

The Basic Rules for Egg Collection

If fertility is proven then fresh eggs will be the secret of your success. Always collect the eggs as soon as you possibly can and set them in the machine, with the eggs marked with the date of collection as well as the date set. Do this as quickly as possible — eggs stored for more than seven to ten days will lose fertility quite rapidly and this can result in some very poor hatches.

Clean the eggs before setting using a mild cleaner. A very gentle wash with Milton steriliser or egg wash is ideal, but under no circumstances leave the eggs in water. They are porous and over time any dirt or bacteria on the outside could work its way inside, harming the developing chick. If you are going to store the eggs, make sure they are kept in

an area where the temperature is likely to remain level at between 13 and 14°C (55.4 and 57.2°F) – not too hot or too cold. Some rooms will always be prone to constant temperature changes but an unused room will most likely remain constant and therefore ideal. Always remember to check on factors such as central heating settings!

Always wait for 24 hours before putting the eggs into the incubator, especially if they are very fresh. Waiting 3 days before setting very fresh eggs is good advice, and turn the eggs at least twice a day prior to setting to make sure the developing embryo does not stick to the shell.

Incubation Settings and Hatching Basics

In my experience problems occur primarily through the operator not adjusting the machine settings correctly; incorrect temperature settings with the heat either too high or too low, or not taking into account room variations can have catastrophic consequences. Incorrect humidity is another major cause of failure, with high humidity producing too wet an environment and too low humidity too dry. If both humidity and temperature settings are wrong then the likelihood of hatching any chicks will be almost zero.

Buying equipment can also be confusing these days as the market is now filled with many wonderful devices, some of which you definitely do need, some which will just make life that bit easier, and others which are probably a complete waste of money, if bought for the wrong reason. An excess of gadgets and knobs is not really necessary for the typical small scale garden keeper who may only have a couple of eggs at the most.

Successful incubation is dependent mainly on a methodical and organised approach to all parts and stages of the process. There is always a need to keep records of all the important dates involved such as when the eggs were collected and when they were set in the incubator. You will also need to know from which pens the eggs were collected if you have more than one. Recording these dates

Marking the eggs ready for incubation.

and times will help you to achieve good results over the coming years as you can learn from your earlier mistakes, and as the results become better, so will your confidence. Over-confidence, however, can often lead to a sloppy approach and failure.

The Incubator Position

An incubator is simply a machine that must be sited in a suitable environment for it to operate correctly and to its full capacity. Placing the incubator in a suitable position is *very* important for achieving the best results and hatches. A stable environment will allow the machine to work to its full capacity as it can be set at an appropriate temperature and will remain there. Centrally heated rooms or any rooms affected by direct sunlight will have fluctuations which could have catastrophic effects on your hatching success as these factors will influence both temperature *and* humidity. Most machines will be unable to compensate for such considerable variations. An ususued bedroom with the radiators turned off would be ideal.

> *Garages, unused bedrooms (with the central heating turned off) or any spare room will normally be suitable, as these will remain at a constant temperature for twenty four hours a day.*

Always allow plenty of ventilation too such as a slightly open window to maintain a good environment. Garden sheds, greenhouses or lean-to type buildings are usually not suitable as they are subject to temperature changes throughout the day and night, and if the sun becomes hot the room temperature can soar, causing the incubator to also become overheated. The same applies

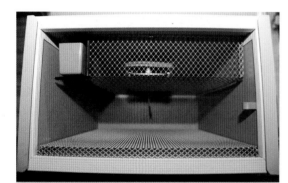

A manual incubator where the eggs have to be turned by hand and lie on the base.

A modern manual incubator turned by moving the cradle back and forth.

Setting up the incubator.

during the colder months as during the day the levels may be fine, but at night they can drop so low that it upsets the incubator settings.

Popular places where people choose to site incubators are often in the kitchen or living room. This is possibly because modern incubators are small, reasonably attractive and have clear tops through which you can watch the whole hatching process. These areas are, however, both subject to constant fluctuations in heat caused by people opening and closing doors, cooking and, of course, the central heating will keep altering the levels constantly as the house thermostat turns the system on and off. Although it may be interesting and exciting to watch the incubation process as it happens, it is far better to make sure that it takes place in a suitable environment for both yourself and the developing embryos. Don't lose sight of your reasons for incubating those eggs – to hatch as many chicks as you can!

Preparation

One single word covers much of the preparation required for any incubator, and that word is 'cleanliness'. Cleaning is of the utmost importance and all traces of dirt must be removed before using the incubator. Dirty incubators are an ideal breeding ground for bacteria and therefore must be cleaned thoroughly before you set any eggs for hatching. Before you start to clean, make the job a lot easier by removing as much of the fitted interior parts as possible; egg trays and humidity trays are straight forward to remove and they can be cleaned easily away from the machine. Give them a good scrub in the kitchen sink, provided this is allowed. Always use a good disinfectant and a hard brush to make sure *all* dirt is removed, and then rinse them thoroughly and allow to dry naturally before replacing them in the incubator.

The interior needs to be cleaned with care as many incubators have electric motors, fans and thermometers etc., all of which should not come into direct contact with water. I have always used

A fully automatic incubator complete with humidity control.

a recommended disinfectant which is suitable for this process and the one I find works best is 'Milton', perhaps better known as a cleaner used for babies' bottles. It is non-corrosive and safe to use – simply dilute it with warm water and clean out all the corners and joints where dirt and bacteria can hide. A hand-held spray is great for this job but again avoid all the electrical parts. To clean any dust and dirt from the fans and motors, use a dry medium bristle brush to brush any dust away. Inside most incubators there is a temperature sensor which hangs down just above the eggs – take great care not to bend or damage this as it is the part of the equipment that keeps the temperature settings level when the machine is running.

A small incubator fitted with an auto turning tray on the base – the eggs are rolled to turn them.

When the inside looks as clean as possible, replace all the trays and other fittings and turn on the incubator. Run it for at least 24 hours to make sure that the cleaning has not disturbed any of the settings, and once you have confirmed this and the temperature inside, then the eggs can be added and you are ready to go.

Fault Finding

The Wrong Temperature/Humidity

Successful hatches are for the most part achieved when the incubator is running at its full potential with the temperature correct and the humidity kept at the correct level throughout the whole of the process.

Running the machine with the temperature too low will result in:

Embryos dying during the early stages of development.

Embryos dying during mid-term development.

Overdue hatching times – too low a temperature will certainly extend these.

Deaths in the shells.

Running the machine with the temperature too high will result in:

Embryos dying during the very earliest stages of development.

Embryos dying during mid-term development.

Very early hatching times with chicks hatching before the yolk sac has been absorbed.

Deaths in the shells.

An incorrect humidity will result in:

Deaths in the shells.

Overdue hatching times.

Chicks hatching very wet and weak.

Clear eggs.

Reasons for poor hatching:

A cockerel not treading.

An infertile male – check the bird for fitness and consider changing the cockerel.

Badly stored or contaminated eggs.

Eggs too old to incubate or stored too long prior to setting – the older an egg, the less chance there is of it hatching successfully.

Chilling in the incubator at an early stage, possibly due to a power failure or incubator fault.

Embryos dying at early or mid stages.

Eggs stored at the wrong temperature prior to setting.

An incubator with internal hot or cold spots.

Poor turning of eggs in the incubator.

Bacteria has built up inside the unit.

The birds are from very closely bred stock, resulting in weak embryos.

Damaged or badly produced eggs.

Too much humidity – reduce the amount of water in the unit.

Too little humidity – increase the amount of water in the unit.

A temperature inside the incubator set either too high or too low.

Early hatching.

The Incubator and Basic Settings

Filling the water tray to control humidity.

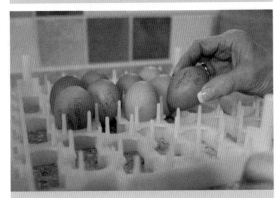

Setting eggs in an auto cabinet incubator tray.

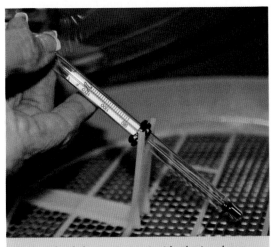

A standard thermometer inside the incubator.

After switching on the incubator and leaving it to stand for twenty four hours, and when you are satisfied that everything is working well with level and steady temperatures, you are finally ready to set your eggs. Most incubators are automatically set to run at 37.5°C, which is the recognised temperature, but I personally prefer 37.8°C, and this variation, although small, has provided me with very good results over the years. The humidity needs to be set at 45% (humidity is measured as the ratio between the actual mass of water vapour present in moist air to the mass of dry air). You would expect to find a humidity level of 35% in a normal household environment, but in most cases water will not need to be added from the first day. If you have an incubator without a humidity gauge (hygrometer) do not worry as there are several on the market, and they are cheap to purchase. By using a gauge you can keep a check to make sure the settings remain at 45% for the first fifteen days and then you can increase it to 55% until day 19 when the reading needs to be increased to 65% for the hatching. To increase the humidity you simply add *warm* water – under no circumstances should you use hot or cold water as this will greatly affect the temperature inside the incubator.

This may all sound a little complicated but it becomes quite straight forward once you get used to the settings.

Setting the eggs will depend on the make and type of incubator you have. Some units have the eggs laid on their sides and they are rolled on the base during the incubation period. There are also those where the setting trays are made of plastic and hold the eggs as if in a normal egg tray. I personally always set the eggs in the trays with the pointed end facing down – this is simply the way I have always set my incubators, although some prefer to set the eggs with the pointed end facing upwards. This decision is down to the individual to choose the best method for them, and if it works then stick with it.

An automatic incubator with removable humidity gauge.

> **When simply storing eggs I always store them with the pointed end upwards, and these practices have probably now just become habit.**

Once all the eggs are in place the machine can be closed and left to level off at the correct settings. Opening it and setting the eggs will have caused a small fluctuation, so keep checking it for the first few hours to make sure everything levels off to precisely what you require.

Once you have completed this it is time to work out the likely hatch date. Start from around 12 hours after setting the eggs to allow the incubator to have reached the correct temperature and humidity, then count the expected days of incubation. As an example, if you set the eggs at 9 o'clock on Monday morning, calculate the time of hatching to be 21 days from 9 o'clock on Monday evening.

The Collection and Storage of Fertile Eggs

When you are ready to start your hatching season and the birds are laying well, the collection and selection of eggs needs to be carried out very carefully. The eggs that you incubate will always need to be carefully selected from the very best shaped eggs with very good quality shells. Do not used deformed, badly shelled or mis-shapen eggs as the result in many cases will be deformed chicks, or chicks which develop but may not survive the full incubation period and end up as what is called 'dead in shell'. You are looking to increase your chances of success by using only the very best prospects.

Date the eggs as you collect them. Use a pencil to mark the date *and* the breed, clearly giving as much information as possible. Marking will help you to make sure that you know exactly how old the eggs are, and which birds they came from.

The information on the eggs gives you an exact record, plus you can also record the information on paper or on a computer as this will help you to identify your best fertile birds, as well as those who are not producing the eggs you need. Good records will certainly be needed to enable you to carry out a proper breeding program where you will need to distinguish between fresher and older eggs and those from your better birds if the venture is to work well.

> *Always use the freshest eggs when setting them for hatching,*

If you have a limited supply of fresh eggs and insufficient to fill your incubator then you may have to take the risk of using slightly older eggs. Try not to set any eggs that are older than 10 days from the day of collection, and when you store them do so at room temperature and at approximately 35% humidity. Do *not* store them in a refrigerator — it may be a way of keeping your eggs fresh, but not for incubation! I store them with the pointed end upwards (the opposite to the way I set them) in either an egg tray or egg box which is tilted slightly to enable me to tip the eggs from side to side at least twice a day to prevent the embryo sticking to the shell. When they are ready to be put into the incubator, give them a final check for any damage, cracks or faults.

Candling and Fertility

Candling eggs is a very important part of the incubation process as it shows the progress and development of the embryo inside the egg. It is quite simple to do too as it involves little more than shining a light through the egg shell. This allows you to see the level of development, and at the later stages the chick actually growing in the egg. Using one of the many custom made candlers that are available today makes the process very easy to do, and there are some excellent hand-held candlers available that are fitted with a high output bulb which penetrates the egg shell very easily. Hand-held candlers are available as either mains or battery powered devices, and both types work perfectly well. When you buy a candler make sure to check that the light is powerful enough

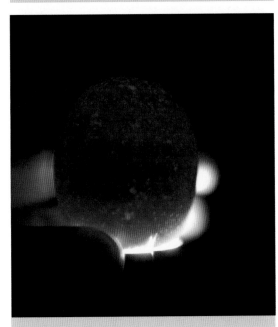

A candling lamp together with an egg that has not formed correctly and is not fertile.

Fertile egg on 7th day.

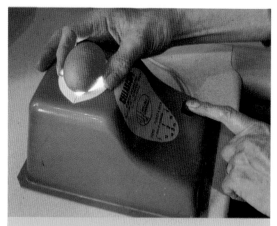

Candling using an electric candler.

A hand-held candler.

A hatched chick, dry and now ready to be moved to the brooder.

to penetrate the shell. This is very important, especially with very dark egg shells as they can often be very hard to check.

When you are checking the embryo it will have the appearance of a distinct black area with what might be described as being like several spider-type legs spreading out around the interior of the shell.

Brooding

After hatching the young chicks will not be able to maintain their correct body heat without our help. To do this and rear the chicks we next have a period referred to as brooding.

Be Prepared

As the end of the incubation time approaches 'the brooder' needs to be prepared and made ready to accept the newly hatched chicks. You must make sure the temperature setting is at the correct level, matching the incubator's 37.5°C. To set the correct heat level, hang the lamp above the brooder and lay a thermometer on the floor, directly beneath the lamp. Leave it in this position for a couple of hours, adjusting the heat level as required by raising or lowering the lamp. This will also make sure that the lamp and bulb are in perfect working order and ready to use. Always have a spare bulb ready just in case you need a replacement at some stage during the brooding period.

Have the food ready too (chick starter crumbs) and a suitable water drinker in which they cannot drown and place them in the brooder, away from the direct heat source.

When chicks are reared naturally the mother will

A home-made brooder using a wardrobe drawer.

Chickens under a small electric hen.

to do, and that is to make your own out of timber which can then be used year after year. Many people who hatch only very small numbers of birds will probably use just a cardboard box with a mesh top and a hanging heat lamp. Once the brooding is completed the box can then be disposed of and a fresh box used for the next batch of chicks.

> *All of these ideas work perfectly well, so whichever one you decide to use makes little difference as long as the temperature is set correctly, the brooder is draught free and there is good ventilation.*

If you do opt for a specially designed brooder it will probably have a built in heat source which is easily adjustable, but with the other options the heat will have to be set by adjusting the height of the heat lamp. This is not difficult but does include a degree of trial and error in the early stages.

The Heat Source

This should really be subtitled 'Getting it right', as it's probably the single most important factor from the point of view of the chicks' crucial early development stage. Heat can be supplied in several ways, but the most popular method is a standard heat lamp fitted with an infrared or white glass bulb. This is suspended above the chicks at a height of approximately 15 inches or higher. This will then give a radius of heat into which the chicks can come and go as they feel comfortable. The temperature from the very first day should be the same or very slightly less than the incubator that they have just left – about 35-37°C – and this level of heat needs to be maintained for the first few days. Then, once the chicks are settling in and

cover the youngsters and provide all the heat needed for them to survive. However, when they are hatched artificially we have to use a method which offers the same results as they would get from their natural mother. Once they have hatched they should be left in the incubator for up to 24 hours to allow them to dry and fluff up. They can then be removed and placed in a suitable place with a supply of heat, food and water.

Brooder Type

There is no set way to brood chicks. You could buy a specially built brooder unit which will have everything you need and will come ready to use. These are excellent but can be quite expensive.

The other option is considerably cheaper and easy

Chicks under a heat lamp in an enclosed brooder.

working you have no visual warning as there is no loss of light, and the only way to check it is by putting your hand underneath the lamp to check the heat – with a standard heat lamp you will lose both heat and light when it ceases to work. You will of course get a reaction from the chicks, but by the time you realise this it might be too late!

There is one advantage to using natural light and a dull emitter bulb, and that is that the chicks respond well to it and you do not tend to get the problem of chicks rolling over backwards as they stare at the light. This is a problem known as 'star gazing', and although reasonably rare it does happen. This is the method I always use myself, but there is no right or wrong here. The decision as to which type of heating you use will simply be your own personal preference.

drinking and feeding successfully, the temperature can be reduced very slightly by about 1°C per week until they are fully feathered. The heat source can then be removed completely.

There is a very simple way of making sure that the heat is set at the correct temperature, and it leaves the chicks to make the point for themselves. If the chicks are cold they will all huddle tightly together directly beneath the heat lamp, and if they are too hot they will be spread out around the very outside of the heat circle, with the centre area totally empty. The ideal situation is when they are evenly spread out in the area beneath the lamp, happily going about their daily routine, and moving in and out of the arc of the lamp as they need to.

The Dull Emitter Bulb

The use of this type of bulb as an alternative has both advantages and disadvantages. It works on the same principle as a standard heat lamp, but supplies heat without light. This type of bulb is made from a type of pot and they are very long lasting bulbs which normally cost quite a lot more than a normal glass infrared bulb. Because the bulb does not give off any light you will have to supply a separate light source, especially if the brooder is dark or in a dark area. The downside to using one of these bulbs is that if the bulb stops

The Heat Pad (or Electric Hen)

This form of rearing young chicks is ideal, provided you have a little more room. Electric hens vary in size and are basically a square heat pad on legs. This allows the chicks to go in and out under the pad for heat as they require. In most cases you will need an additional light source, as the electric hen supplies heat only. The cost is greater than with either of the bulb systems but they last for many years which certainly makes them worthwhile in the long term. Adjusting the heat is simple – you just raise or lower the heat pad using the screws on each leg, but there are recent models which are now fitted with a switch that you turn to adjust the heat, very similar to a dimmer switch that you might use in the house.

Feeding

From the first day feed only chick starter crumbs. Put them in a low sided feeder or tray, and remember that they have no mother present to teach them what to do, so it is a good idea to sprinkle the crumbs from about 6 inches above the brooder floor quite close to the chicks. This will get their attention and they will most likely start to peck and feed almost at once. Keep checking to

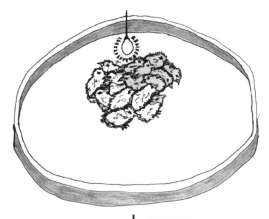

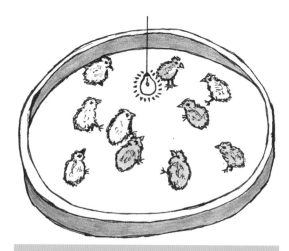

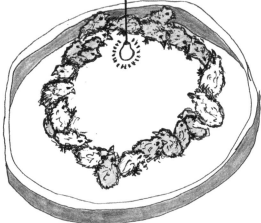

Observe the behaviour of chicks in the brooder to confirm the correct heat levels.

Top left: The chicks are huddled together directly under the heat lamp – this shows they are too cold.
Bottom left: The chicks are spread around outside the heat circle – this shows it is too hot and the lamp is too low.
Above: The chicks are spread out evenly and active – this is the ideal level of heat.

make sure that there is always enough feed available and that all the chicks are feeding and looking healthy.

Depending on the development of the chicks they should be moved on to growers' pellets at around six to eight weeks old. Do not feed them scraps and treats as the chick crumbs and growers' pellets will contain all the ingredients needed to raise healthy birds.

Water

Chicks have a natural tendency to seek out water. Sadly over the years I have seen so many chicks in brooders drowned in water drinkers which are either too deep or open topped. You cannot allow this to happen and it is certainly very easy to prevent. There are chick fonts and drinkers

for sale that are very shallow and narrow lipped. They are not expensive, and they will prevent any chicks from drowning. You can also use an existing drinker, provided that you prevent the chicks from getting into the deeper rim. Fill the drinker with water and then fill the rim with pebbles all the way round. This will allow the chicks' beaks access to the water, but at the same time it will stop them getting into the rim.

Adding a very small quantity of cider vinegar from about four to six weeks is also a good idea as it helps to keep the chicks' guts clean and protects them from internal parasites.

Bedding

Never use straw as it is awkward for the chicks, especially at such an early age. It always looks

The way these chicks are sprawled out around the edge suggests excessive heat.

OK when checked out from the top, but after a while in the brooder if you look underneath it will be damp and mouldy. This leads to respiratory problems later. Use dust free shavings wherever possible, and replace them regularly. Chicks, like all chickens, need to be as clean and dry as possible to reduce the likelihood of outbreaks of disease.

Problems and Diseases during Brooding

Keeping the chicks in a very clean, dry environment will help to prevent most problems from even starting, but there are a few that may arise, and the following is a list of the ones to be aware of:

Coccidiosis is one of the worst yet most common problems in the early life of a chick, but is easy to spot due to blood in the faeces and very lethargic birds. It is a worm infestation and is spread by damp, poor sanitation, dirty drinking water and overcrowding. Treatment is available but only from your vet. Keeping young chicks clean and dry is the best way to prevent it. When it occurs there will usually be a number of fatalities.

Parasites including lice and red mite should be checked for at least two or three times a week, especially if you are using a brooder which has been used before. A thorough cleaning and disinfecting prior to re-use will help to prevent and control this problem. Both mite and lice will weaken chicks, and this makes them more susceptible to a variety of illnesses that would not normally affect healthy chicks. Red mite is particularly dangerous at this stage and will kill young chicks.

Feather pecking is normally the result of overcrowding, boredom, too much light, poor nutrition or mite or lice infestations. It can be hard to control once it begins and needs to be eliminated quickly as it can lead to vent picking and cannibalism, both of which *will* be fatal. If you are using a method of brooding with no light source i.e. a dull emmiter or electric hen, then it is possible to turn off the light at night. Putting the birds in total darkness will help to control the problem. If

A chick that has just hatched.

you are using an infrared bulb system then turning off the light is clearly not an option as both heat and light are from one and the same source. It is very important that birds under constant light have plenty of space, and this, in most cases, will prevent a pecking problem. If you do encounter this problem there are some anti-pecking creams and sprays that can be used – simply apply them to the affected areas on a bird and this will act as a deterrent and stop any future pecking.

Pasted vent (sometimes referred to as 'sticky bum') tends to arise as a result of either too much or not enough heat or light. It usually happens between the ages of 0-10 days and is due to the chicks becoming chilled at an early age. It results in a very messy vent area.

Splayed legs is a potentially serious problem that can often be avoided. It is sometimes caused by incorrect humidity during the incubation period, but the most common cause is simply that when the chicks hatch they are left on too smooth a surface where they cannot get a grip. This results in the legs, which at this stage are not yet strong, splaying, and the result can be permanent disability. Avoiding the problem is very easy – keep checking the humidity at the incubation stage and make sure the floor in the incubator or the hatch tray has either a mesh or material floor to give the birds extra traction. This also applies to the brooder as they need to be able to stand normally until their legs strengthen. Occasionally splayed legs can be corrected by tying the legs loosely together, but results vary, and in many cases the treatment does not work.

Twisted or crooked toes are usually the result of breeding problems or temperatures being set either too high or too low in the incubator. A further cause can be the incorrect setting of the heat lamp in the brooder at a very early stage in the chick's development (see page 154).

Star gazing is the result of chicks standing and staring straight up into the sky. They usually shake their heads slightly and some even roll over backwards, eventually becoming unable to stand normally. It is very rare that a bird recovers from this problem. The cause is *encephalamasia* and

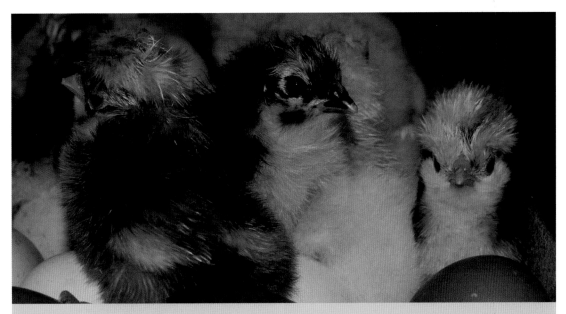

Chicks drying out and fluffing up nicely.

the only usual course of action is to dispose of any affected chicks.

Respiratory infections can also arise due to unsanitary conditions, overcrowding, a lack of ventilation, exposure to adult birds and damp bedding. Good management at this early stage should prevent the problem from occurring.

There are a number of egg-transmitted diseases too, including *adenovirus*; *aspergillosis*; avian *encephalomyelitis*; fowl typhoid: infectious bronchitis; infectious *synvitis*; lymphoid *leucosis*; *mycoplasma gallisepticum*; *mycoplasma meleagridis*; various forms of salmonella including *Pullorum* and yolk sac infection. Fortunately these are all very rare occurrences.

Natural Brooding

Quite often you will hear people say "We thought we had lost that bird, yet here she is with a brood of chicks following close behind." It is very common for a hen to actually find and make her own nest and set up home – and they often do it in some of the most inaccessible and unsuitable places. If you keep both hens and a cock and have a female bird that appears to show broody signs, make sure to keep a close eye on her and try and help her to nest in a suitable and safe place.

A Broody Coop

Keeping chicks safe once they have hatched can be a problem, especially if your birds are free range. By using a broody coop it will help to keep both the adult bird and chicks confined in a safer environment until they reach a suitable age to be allowed to roam more freely. The broody coop can be anything from an old box to a specially constructed coop with a small enclosed run attached. This will simply enable the mother to complete her role and bring up the chicks safely, and hopefully leave behind her broody stage too.

Detail of broody box showing rounded corners to prevent crushing.

Chick drinker with narrow lip to prevent drowning.

Three Poland chicks at about 8 weeks old. Left to Right: A White Crested Frizzle, a Chamois and a Gold Laced.

Natural Incubation

This is the term used to describe a hen mating naturally, laying her eggs and sitting on them until they hatch, then rearing the chicks as nature intended. Hens will often go broody and sit the eggs for the full period, which in the case of chickens is 21 days.

As with almost everything, there are both good and bad points regarding natural incubation, and these are as follows:

The Good Points

Natural rearing always seems to produce good, strong healthy chicks.

The chicks build up a natural immunity to disease.

Virtually no work is involved for the keeper (except regular checks for insects and cleaning out nests etc.).

The hen rears her own brood, from hatching to adult.

The Bad Points

(These relate principally to a broody hen sitting eggs which are not her own.)

Broody hens are not always ready to sit when you might have fertile eggs ready to incubate.

Hens can *and do* walk away from clutches for no apparent reason.

A broody hen will collect *all* the eggs laid in her area and try to sit every one of them.

Sitting birds can *and do* attract red mite, which can kill both hen and chicks if not taken care of.

The actual hatch date can be a little hard to work out, unless all the eggs are marked on the date laid.

Natural Broody Breeds

Certain breeds of poultry are what is classed as a non-sitter. This means exactly what it says on the tin, as they say. They will *lay* eggs but will *not* hatch their own young. Check with the breed before buying, especially if you would like to brood your own chicks using a broody hen.

Breeds classed as ideal broodies are the Sussex, Rhode Island Red and Welsummer, but the most successful of all is the Silkie, which can be crossed with a Light Sussex to create the ideal broody hen. This cross is the perfect solution as it also produces sex-linked chicks at just one day old.

Using the natural system is preferred by many breeders, but incubation using an incubator has really become more popular today. The units are now extremely reliable and easy to operate, and they give you a considerable level of control. This allows you to hatch as many eggs (or as few) as you require, and also lets you set the eggs at certain times to give a very accurate idea of hatching dates. This effectively cuts out much of the guess work, and also removes any potential insect problems associated with natural sitting.

Houdan chicks fluffing up nicely.

Seasonal Chores

The Healthy Hens Handbook

Seasonal Chicken Chores

Whatever the time of year, keeping poultry correctly is an ongoing task with no end; it's a bit like painting the Tay Bridge – as you finish at one end, it's time to start again at the other. Chickens need continual management, both to keep them in good health and condition, and also to provide a decent quality of life. Your birds, in turn, will provide you with a good supply of eggs and, in some cases, meat too. For this arrangement to work at its best your birds need to be in top condition. Laying eggs is part of their natural process, and healthy birds will lay eggs regularly.

Each time of year brings with it new challenges for the poultry keeper. Winter is obviously the worst time of year as the elements are against both birds and keeper. Freezing weather brings with it many problems, ranging from frozen water supplies to illness caused by the damp, cold conditions, and is also hard on poultry sheds and coops, in particular wooden ones, which will effectively rot away if not protected. Carrying out routine repairs and maintenance during winter is always far more difficult than when the weather is warm, dry and calm – many jobs are therefore put off until the weather improves, making spring a busy time for the conscientious keeper. This is usually the time when catching up and putting right the damage done by the bad winter weather takes place, but it is also the time of year when birds start to reproduce, and as the breeding season begins in earnest, the workload can become hectic for anyone looking to breed from their existing flock.

For any keeper with a sizable flock, carrying out what can sometimes amount to major repairs at the same time as preparing for new young stock can be quite a task, so rather than ignoring many overdue tasks, always select and complete the most important ones by prioritising – but don't forget to take at least some time out to enjoy this most rewarding of seasons too. For most small scale keepers this should not be too great a problem as maintaining a single coop should not present too great a workload.

During the summer you can catch up on any remaining tasks and also begin to prepare for the autumn – and although you might not like to think about it, the oncoming winter. Summer also brings its own unique challenges such as excess heat, a greater likelihood of insect infestations and, of course, for many of us it is the time to go on holiday. This comparatively ordinary exercise (for the non-chicken keeper) can create considerable problems as getting someone reliable in to care for the birds while you are away can be difficult. As the birds rely entirely on their keeper for sustenance, you will need someone conscientious to rely on who will make sure your birds are well catered for.

Chicken keeping really is a year round occupation, and one that certainly has its ups and downs, but is at the same time extremely enjoyable and rewarding. I know very few people who have regretted the commitment, once made, but it does require a degree of self-discipline to get the most out of it for both you and your birds. I have, over the following sections, tried to outline the seasonal chores, but they do inevitably overlap, with many tasks repeated on a weekly rather than monthly basis. If some things are done a day or too late no-one will complain, as long as shelter and security are good, cleanliness maintained and a good supply of both feed and water are made available at all times.

Spring

Check for weather damage on hinges.

Due to the cold and damp of winter, spring tasks often include a fair amount of repairing and/or replacing any damage to housing, fence posts, gateposts and wire mesh. It is vital that these repairs are carried out to keep your birds safe and secure. Replace or re-set any fencing posts that have come loose, make sure all the hinges, bolts and any wire mesh on the housing and any runs are all secure, and check that they have not corroded during the winter weather as this could allow the housing or run to be accessed by predators. Throughout the winter you will no doubt have done a number of temporary repairs, but as the weather improves it's now time do a proper and more permanent job.

> *Always remember that it only needs a very small hole or some loose wire for a fox or other predator to gain access.*

External Housing Repairs

The first thing to check after winter is the felt on the roof of the chicken housing. Felt is always vulnerable in bad weather, especially if it is a few years old. The heat of the summer months dries it out, at which point it goes really hard and brittle, and then when the weather becomes wet and freezing, it begins to crack and split, and very soon starts to leak. If it is not repaired quickly it will just break away in large patches and fall off the roof at the first sign of wind. If the felt is damaged it is always better to remove *all* the old felt and replace it with new rather than patch it up. Patching it up is of course the cheaper option, but it will most likely be a false economy. There are different grades of thickness of felt and I always use a thicker gauge which is considerably more heavy duty than that fitted by most shed builders. Although felt is guaranteed, I have never actually known anyone

Be on the look out for any wood that has taken a battering over the winter.

who has claimed for it not lasting its claimed full lifespan.

There are other types of roofing such as onduline sheeting which will easily fasten onto your existing roof. If the felt is damaged this may be an ideal time to replace it with a longer lasting material. Onduline is corrugated, so you will have to make sure that the housing is inaccessible to small predators and vermin via the gaps caused by the undulations in the material. Once in place, however, it will last for many years.

Wooden coops will need treating with some sort of protective coating. As most of today's treatments are chemical free this is a job which should be carried out regularly once a year. There are several different products on the market at your local DIY store which are recommended for use in animal housing, so you will have a good choice of both material and colour to suit.

Check for any signs of rot and damage to the housing, especially behind hinges which can hold water, causing the wood to rot and weakening the security of the hinge. You may not see it at

first glance but a predator might. If in doubt press forcefully on any wooden panels about which you are uncertain – Mr Fox will certainly not be gentle when *he* comes calling!

Internal Housing Repairs

Much of your post-winter chores inside the housing will involve cleaning. This is normally classed as daily or weekly maintenance, but during winter what you can do is often severely limited due to the dampness and the inability to dry off a coop if it has been power washed. It is therefore worth giving the housing a once a year major overhaul inside, and to do this you should remove *all* internal parts of the coop, including perches, nest boxes, droppings trays, feeders and drinkers – literally anything that is removable. Scrub and disinfect everything using a good quality recommended product and scrape off *all* the perches. If the dirt is too bad and impossible to remove then replace them as required. Using a power washer is a great way to clean the inside of a coop, but it needs to be done on a warm, dry day as the housing needs to be dry when the chickens return to roost – housing them in a wet coop is a

Don't overlook any fencing that needs replacing.

bad idea, even if it is clean. With spring, however, the hours of daylight increase and birds roost later, giving you a little more time to get the job done properly and the coop dry.

A major cleaning process should be carried out at least once a year, but there should also be a weekly clean together with a thorough treatment against mites and insects and a disinfecting of the housing to keep it in good order throughout the year – neglect this essential routine and I assure you your workload will increase and the welfare of the birds will suffer.

Once the coop is dry, and before the birds are allowed to return, spray the inside with a good red mite treatment, making sure you get the product into *all* the nooks and crannies. Once you have completed this, use BioDri or Stalosan disinfectant on the floor of the coop and in the nest boxes before putting down any clean bedding of dust free shavings. These products will help to dry out any remaining dampness, kill any bugs, lice and their eggs, sterilise the environment *and* eliminate ammonia fumes, which are a major cause of respiratory disease in poultry. This will leave the poultry house smelling fresh again after the winter

months, when it may have been occupied for up to sixteen hours each night during the long hours of darkness in winter.

Under no circumstances should you use common domestic cleaners.

Most supermarket products suitable for the kitchen or toilet are definitely not acceptable as they can in some cases be toxic to animals, and may create fumes which could have an adverse effect on livestock. Use only products which are designed and licensed for animal and poultry welfare, and always read the instructions, or ask the supplier if you are uncertain.

Outside Runs and Pens

If these are grass areas they may well have become mud baths by spring. It is almost impossible to do any significant maintenance on the ground areas of poultry runs during the short hours of winter light and the area may well have become 'sour' by spring. If you are able to re-site the housing and run, or if you have done so regularly during the winter months, it will be of great benefit now. As the weather gets warmer any 'soured' patch will begin to smell, and to prevent this you will need to skim at least a couple of inches off the soil surface. This can be disposed of on the compost heap.

A rotavator would be a useful tool as you will need to turn the area over. Afterwards, leave the ground area more or less level, and the birds will have great fun digging and hunting for any insects, and will complete the levelling process very quickly. I always try to turn the soil at least once a month and add a sprinkling of BioDri each time to help freshen up the area. The digging up and turning over of the run is also an effective way of helping to prevent parasites and disease on what may have become an infected area through constant occupation by the birds.

Drinkers and Feeders

Freezing weather may well have damaged and split plastic feeders or drinkers which you will need to replace. Thoroughly clean and disinfect all drinkers and feeders, and continue to do so regularly as part of your disease prevention regime. Dirty equipment harbours disease, so the effort will be worthwhile, and if you use an automatic drinker check it out for possible ice damage which could eventually cause it to flood. I always take mine to pieces and reassemble them so I know for certain that they are in good working order.

Rubbish Clearance

Disposing of dirty bedding is always an unpleasant chore, and dependent on the amount the local tip may not be too welcoming either – not a problem for the small scale keeper though, who can usually throw it on the compost heap. Sometimes it might seem easier to leave it for later, especially when it is freezing, snowing and blowing a gale, but dirty

Applying BioDri in the coop to prevent disease.

A very clean coop after a blast with the power washer.

bedding is a great nesting place for rodents and all other manner of vermin. Instead, keep on top of it over the winter months by putting some on your compost heap, and if there is occasionally more than you can handle, see if the local allotment society or a local farmer can dispose of it constructively. It is also a good time to walk around the housing area and any sheds, clearing out all manner of rubbish, and removing anything which may be even vaguely tempting to a rodent in search of a home.

While clearing out, use the opportunity to check for any signs of rats or mice, looking for signs of digging round the housing and any sheds, especially underneath, or gnawing around openings and pop-holes. The signs are usually easy to see. Check out any dark, hard to get to areas, and look for a nest of feathers or other soft material. This is an ideal time to review your traps and bait too to make sure you are in control of any rodent problem, both for your own health

and that of the birds. Permanent traps and or bait are recommended all year round to keep the situation in check, but keeping the area around the housing clean and tidy will make it less desirable for vermin, and also make it easier for you to spot any new and unwanted arrivals.

SPRING 'TO DO' CHECK LIST

Make the most of the longer and hopefully drier days to carry out an inspection of the coop, both inside and out.

Check the condition of any felt on the roof and repair or replace as necessary.

Check for and repair any structural damage to the housing.

Check and replace any damaged hinges, bolts or latches on the housing.

Check your fencing and carry out any repairs where needed.

Give the housing a complete spring clean using a power washer if you've got one. Make sure you choose a fine spring day so that it dries out before they go to roost.

Check all feeders and drinkers for signs of wear and tear and replace them if necessary.

Remember to give the rest of the area around the housing the spring clean treatment too, removing rubbish and other potential nesting spots for vermin.

Summer

A Black Silkie bantam

Applying mite powder.

I am not sure whether summer chores are simply preferable to those required in early spring, when you are effectively clearing up after the winter mess, or if it is just that the better weather and longer days make us all feel better. Each new season has its own unique tasks, and in summer these can include setting up this year's breeding pens, getting the birds prepared and fit for the summer's egg production, and, last but not least, preparing for any forthcoming summer shows and exhibitions if you choose to show your birds.

The preparation of the birds and their housing is absolutely critical at this time of year as it can and will affect much of the remaining year's results for any poultry breeders and exhibitors.

> **Whether or not you show or breed, this is the perfect time to give your birds a complete check.**

The days are long and the weather is usually better, the birds will probably be dry and somewhat cleaner than in spring or winter, so this is a good opportunity to give them a visual once over, and to tackle any day to day maintenance. Continue your regime of regularly clearing out any waste or rubbish, and continue with a policy of zero tolerance of untidiness around the housing.

The whole of the area from the actual poultry unit to the ground the unit stands on, plus the area in which the birds run, all need to be checked regularly. If the housing can be moved around to fresh ground then all the better, but if this is not possible then a good and thorough clean of the surface of the run, whether it is on soft or hard ground, will be a good idea. This is a time when infestations thrive, and without constant action from the poultry keeper problems will build up rapidly. If you really want to be certain of interrupting the lifecycle of these parasites then completely digging the run over if the birds are foraging on soil or grass will be useful.

Just because the weather is now better it is no excuse for not using your eyes to check over the housing. The weather will not be as destructive, but countering wear and tear is a constant battle for the conscientious poultry keeper.

More important though is the regular cleaning

regime. Undeniably cleaning poultry units has never been one of the more pleasant tasks – it is a dirty and dusty business, but it has to be done. Both inside and outside should have any dust, cobwebs and droppings removed, and to carry out this operation you should put on old work clothes or overalls, and using a dust filter mask for protection is a sensible precaution. If you are doing this on a regular weekly basis then the removal of *all* the fittings is not required, but a good dose of red mite treatment, a good louse and insect powder and a good disinfectant will be essential, especially if the weather is warm, and even more so if it is damp too. The strange changing weather which often characterizes our summers means we seem to have an increase in mite and louse infestations each year, so over the warmer months spraying both the inside and outside of the unit must be an ongoing process which needs to be done on a weekly basis if they are to be kept under control. The one really essential tool is a good, sharp hand-held scraper, and if your housing is large there are scrapers available which come on something similar to a broom handle – these will make life much easier.

If your housing is large then cleaning this way means you may well be spending at least some time on your hands and knees to make sure all dirt and droppings are removed, and at this time of year any residues are likely to be solid as summer temperatures will dry out droppings rapidly. These will usually harbour insects, but especially their eggs, creating a potential disease problem. Once you have scraped the floor clean, sweep the inside of the coop well with a stiff brush, and if you have an old vacuum cleaner available it will make the job easier, especially for cobwebs and any dust in the corners, which is often difficult to disturb with a brush alone. If you only have the one and it is reasonably new then a really good sweep will have to do, but be sure to wear a mask – a disease such as aspergillosis and a number of others which affect poultry can affect humans too!

Red mite after feeding.

The Healthy Hens Handbook

Red mite hiding in the legs of a plastic drinker.

External Cleaning

The best ways to clean the outside of a poultry unit are with either a really stiff brush dipped in disinfectant or with a power washer. Make sure you remove any cobwebs and hardened bird droppings (often those of wild birds, in this instance!) which are stuck to the exterior as they are always ideal hiding places for insects. Ensure that all joints and edges are cleaned out thoroughly, and if there are any signs of insect infestation, spray the whole of the shed liberally to make sure the problem is kept under control. Bear in mind too that just because you cannot see an infestation it does not mean that the problem does not exist. A keeper can become complacent, but constant checking and maintenance is needed all year round, including during winter months when they remain largely dormant, if the problem is to be controlled.

Treating the Timber

It is a good idea to take advantage of any dry spells to treat the timber of any wooden housing units. This will help it to withstand the ravages of the next winter. If the wood from which it is made is pressure treated then it will not normally be necessary, but for most flat pack units designed to hold a small number of birds it will be advisable, and on an annual basis as today's treatments are mostly water-based as legislation has now banned many of the chemicals which, many years ago, gave them their longevity.

When treating a poultry unit on the inside, always use a product that will cause no health problems for any birds housed in it. The ideal product needs to be non-toxic and suitable for sheds and fencing, and with no residues of harmful fumes left behind which could linger and harm the birds over a period of time. Cuprinol is one of today's market leaders and comes in a wide range of colours to suit all garden environments.

SUMMER 'TO DO' CHECK LIST

If you can move the coop and any run to another spot do so - this will allow the ground to recover.

Ensure you have in place a weekly cleaning regime to keep on top of mites and any other pests.

Take advantage of any dry weather to treat the timber or even paint your coop.

Check drinking water several times each day to make sure there is always sufficient fresh supply available.

Make sure you take time to enjoy the summer too – your birds certainly will.

Autumn

Felt in desperate need of replacement before winter begins.

Autumn should be viewed by the conscientious chicken keeper as being a less harsh stage of winter, when preparation is still considerably easier and less unpleasant than during the coming months. Anything you don't do in the autumn you will have to do during winter, irrespective of how bad the weather might be, when maintenance to housing might be impractical or downright impossible. So as the summer comes to an end, begin your preparations for the oncoming winter weather.

The priority at this time should be the housing and any pens or runs, as when winter really sets in it will prevent general repairs from being carried out due to the damp state of any wooden housing, and the need for the birds to be under shelter on a more regular basis than in the warmer months. At this time of year plastic housing, or the newly available recycled materials, are easier to deal with, as rotting is not usually a problem, so leaks and security problems due to small holes are less likely to arise. Do not become complacent though – there are always access points for the determined predator, so keep looking and deal promptly with anything that looks like an easy access point. An additional advantage of plastic or recycled material is that as it is non-porous, it will dry out much quicker if washed on a reasonably fine day, so you can still get out the hose on occasion.

The birds should still be examined regularly and this is a good time to make sure beaks and nails are trimmed and lice and mite treated with the correct sprays or powders, because even though the weather is colder, these insects will remain alive on the birds due to their body heat. Even during the coldest time of year they can still breed and increase in numbers if left unattended. For further advice see the Chicken M.O.T. section in the appendices on page 204.

Give all feeders and drinkers a thorough clean and disinfect them. If automatic drinkers are being used make sure filters are clean and unblocked, and any turn-off valves are working as they will be needed when temperatures drop below freezing.

AUTUMN 'TO DO' CHECK LIST

Prepare the coop for the onslaught of winter by checking the roof, hinges, bolts and the wood itself for any signs of decay. Replace any weak points and consider replacing any felt with onduline or a similar long-lasting material.

Conduct a thorough M.O.T. on your chickens to ensure that they are strong enough to weather the extremes of the forthcoming winter. Consider a tonic or extra vitamins for any birds going through the moult.

Winter

Frost damage is clearly visible on both the wattle and comb of this bird.

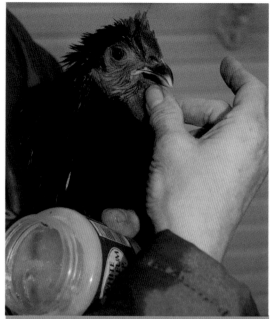

Apply Vaseline to the wattle and comb to prevent frost damage.

Winter is the month which probably puts the most stress on any chicken keeper, but perhaps less so on the birds themselves, as most breeds tend to be quite hardy. Each year though, chicken keepers agonise over the problem of trying to decide on the best way to prepare for the anticipated wet and cold weather expected over the winter months.

There are certain breeds that will need special attention due to their feather type and breed characteristics, but as a general rule most birds will suffer no ill effects, even in very cold temperatures. The most important thing is to make sure the birds are provided with adequate cover for protection against the weather. The housing needs to be kept dry and free from draughts, but with adequate ventilation, and this is especially important in the areas were the birds roost overnight. Bedding also needs to be kept fresh, dry and clean, which will help to prevent disease and infection. This will mean regularly replacing the bedding due to the inevitable wet and muddy weather, especially if your birds are free range and left to forage.

There will always need to be a supply of fresh, clean water, and a regular supply of fresh, dry food. If temperatures do go below freezing then, as in summer, you must make regular checks on the water supply, especially if you use an automatic system. There are a series of common sense checks that you should carry out both *before* and *during* the winter period, and these are as follows:

Checking for Visible Signs of Problems

Winter can be a difficult time, but if some regular basic work is carried out it can save you both time and money, and will also make sure that your birds remain in prime condition. Carrying out a basic sight check of the birds from a distance will allow you to see them in a natural state without disturbing them, and this will help you to pick out any that are looking under the weather or showing signs of illness or distress. If you are new to keeping chickens this may be a little difficult if you are not sure what to look for, but it becomes easier as you get used to the way they behave as they go about their daily routine. Most birds are acquired

Dehydration is still a potential problem in winter. Be sure to check the water.

when held, and carry out the checks in a prompt and business-like manner.

While you have the bird in hand, check for signs of illness, damage, injury, mites and any other insect problems, as this can be done quite easily. Such checks done regularly will help to prevent many of the problems from which birds can suffer during winter months.

Are there any Signs of Disease?

Check for eye infections, permanently closed eyes or discharge from the nose, as these are all potential signs of illness. Look also for signs of wheezing, gasping and sneezing, all of which may be signs of a cold. Listening to the birds as they roost is a good and non-invasive way of checking their breathing. Any signs of infection will most likely be heard as a rattling sound as a poorly bird tries to breathe.

Do the Birds Look Physically Fit?

Combs and wattles should be a bright red colour; this will mean that a bird is most likely healthy. If they are pale or damaged then further checks should be made. Extreme cold can affect both combs and wattles, with birds occasionally suffering from frostbite. In *very* cold weather gently rub in a little Vaseline. This should protect them against extreme cold first thing in the morning. Eyes should be bright, and birds alert and active, with smooth and even breathing. The vent area should be clean, without swelling and free from insect infestation – if this is not the case a good dusting of insect powder is required. The stomach and crop should show no sign of swelling. Check the feathers too – any problems could be a sign of moult or something more serious such as feather pecking due to boredom over long nights in the coop. This could develop into cannibalism if not dealt with. Any sign of bleeding should certainly prompt very swift action from you.

during spring or summer so this should give you enough time to recognise 'normal' behaviour. It is impossible to over emphasise the importance of knowing your birds when it comes to spotting any problems at an early stage, when action can usually be taken.

Do Your Birds Look Healthy?

If any of your birds seem overly lethargic or look very sorry for themselves then to check them further you will need to catch them for a proper close up examination. This examination is often best done by two people, with one person holding the bird securely, or by wrapping the bird in an old towel to help keep it under control – a struggling bird will always be very hard to examine.

The relative ease or difficulty of catching birds can depend on the breed, but it is better to carry out the task in the evening when the birds are settling down, as this will save you much chasing and frustration in the pen.

Handle birds with care, once you have caught them. Most are reasonably easy to handle, but some breeds can be hard to control, and it is these ones that often suffer from stress. Reduce any problems by making sure each bird feels secure

Take care not to leave your birds vulnerable to chills.

Damp and muddy conditions can soon lead to hard balls forming on the claws.

Checking for Insects

Insects are *always* a problem irrespective of the season, and winter is no exception. With birds in the coop for long times during the extended hours of darkness, temperatures soar and in a likely damp environment it is very much business as usual for bugs, lice and red mite. Lice and mite can often be seen in the feathers around the vent. Anything that looks like cotton wool on feather quills could be mite egg cases, and these will need to be treated. Anything that looks like grey dust or cigarette ash may be northern mite, especially around the vent, the base of the tail or the nape of the neck.

Checking inside the Housing

The main insect problem will undoubtedly be red mite, the most dangerous of all insects for chickens; even as temperatures drop they still lurk inside the housing. Numbers and levels of activity do undoubtedly decrease during winter months, but they are still there, coming out to feed off the birds during the night. In fact birds are a real magnet for insects at this time of year due to their body heat, so continued vigilance and treatment remain essential. Remember too that mite are able to lie dormant for very considerable lengths of time, so the problem never goes away. Many keepers cease treating the coop during winter – this is a big mistake, and one you will pay for as warmer weather returns! Products such as Diatom (diatomaceous earth) used around the coop and under the bedding will help to keep at bay both these and other insects, and used together with BioDri, will keep the winter coop in a reasonable condition. A spot type insect treatment will be useful too, so consult with your vet for a recommended one.

Legs and Feet

Legs and feet are often neglected, but during winter birds are often walking in mud, and combined with droppings this can compact and harden on the feet. Scaly mite is also something to keep an eye out for, often seen as raised scales on the legs and a whitish crusty residue. It is caused by an insect which burrows under the scales, infecting the flesh and causing great discomfort for the birds. Any visible sign will require treatment using a spray, followed by the use of Vaseline as the leg mends. This will suffocate any remaining mites.

Worming

Checking for internal parasites is difficult, but take appropriate precautions by checking on the birds' droppings. Signs of blood, yellow diarrhoea or very runny, watery droppings should give cause for concern. Normal healthy droppings consists of a dark solid part and a white section – the dark part is the faeces and the white the urine. A dirty, wet and soiled vent can also be an indication of worm infestation. Internal parasites (endoparasites) such as worms are always a serious threat to birds, but worming regularly is comparatively simple. Wormers can be liquid mixed into drinking water (*Solubenol* given every three to four months) or powder (Flubenvet given once every six months in feed) or ready mixed in with feed pellets (usually Flubenvet). Verm-X, a natural product used by many organic producers, is also available as a wormer supplied in both liquid and pellet form. When using any of these products, follow the manufacturer's instructions.

> *Keeping runs and coops as dry and clean as possible (a difficult job in winter!) is one of the most important tasks in getting your birds safely through to the next season.*

Making sure the birds are kept in clean and dry conditions with fresh bedding will help to keep them in a healthy condition, and avoid leaving them to forage on old, dirty ground as this is a breeding place for parasites. Moving runs and regular worming will help prevent a serious build up, and cider vinegar just twice a week will help to reduce internal problems and enhance the birds' health. Maintaining good ventilation but without draughts is essential in a night time coop full of chickens. Adding extra vitamins will be advisable too, with a general supplement once or twice a week.

Winter does always seems like a difficult time of the year, but in my experience birds just seem to get on with doing what they normally do. They can look a little bit miserable at times, but so can we in winter. If you carry out these checks periodically and guarantee that their water supply remains fresh and not frozen, and their food fresh and dry, they should come out pretty healthy at the other end when spring arrives. Just don't worry, and try to avoid handling your birds excessively to check them or the stress you may create could be more damaging than the worst of the winter weather.

WINTER 'TO DO' CHECK LIST

Make sure the drinking water isn't frozen over.

Keep on top of worming – now is the perfect time as egg production usually dies back.

Your birds will spend more time in their housing due to the longer nights, so make sure that bedding is kept clean.

Check ventiliation – even on the coldest of nights do not be tempted to close all airways into the coop.

Check the birds' feet and legs for build ups of mud which can compact and harden.

Keep an eye out too for signs of scaly mite and any other likely infestation. Act promptly if you notice anything out of the ordinary.

Appendices

The Healthy Hens Handbook

An A-Z of Poultry Ailments

Avian Influenza

This now has to be the best known poultry disease on the planet. It is an airborne virus that affects a bird's respiratory system in the same way as we humans might catch a cold. The outward signs include ruffled feathers, droopiness, *cyanosis* (a purplish-blue colouring in the comb and wattles), diarrhoea, a discharge from the nostrils which 'may be bloody', problems breathing, not being able to walk properly or steadily and, of course, an increased number of deaths in the flock.

Although there have been a reported number of infections that have been transmitted to humans, the numbers still remain very small as the level of involvement with birds required to catch it is very, very high, but the threat does remain with us, so caution is always advisable in terms of contact, and this means protection such as a mask when doing certain jobs and good hygiene, which is often as simple as washing your hands well after dealing with birds.

Of course there are a number of different varieties of avian flu and in the low pathogenic mild cases the birds will recover, and normally without serious loss, but in the high pathogenic form the results will be far more serious, with the likely loss of birds being almost 100%, and if they are not killed by the disease they will most likely be slaughtered to prevent further infection. Always take precautions while dealing with birds, and bear in mind that because the main source of infection is from wild birds, bio security is very important to both reduce and prevent any disease. At this time the only outbreak in the UK was at an intensive turkey farm in Norfolk with birds brought in from outside the UK. Any imposition of greater security requirements could have an immense effect on free range poultry and its continued existence.

Avian Tuberculosis

Tuberculosis is a serious wasting disease that

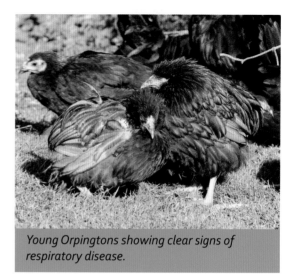

Young Orpingtons showing clear signs of respiratory disease.

affects all species of birds, and especially domestic poultry. Birds of all ages can be affected, with older birds usually appearing to be more vulnerable. The symptoms are a gradual wasting of the muscles and birds looking ruffled, dull and lifeless, with drooping wings and diarrhoea. The usual outcome is a culling of the entire flock.

Blackhead

This is a disease that primarily affects young turkeys, and although chickens seem to be quite resistant to the disease, they can become carriers of the infection. The correct name of the disease is *histomoniasi* and it is caused by a microscopic protozoan called *Histomonas meleagridi*. It is normally transmitted by water, feed and droppings, but eggs infected with the parasitic worm can also be a source of the infection.

Signs of the disease are birds looking dull and usually standing alone with ruffled feathers, and droppings can be a very bright yellow. If not treated quickly the death rate will most likely be very high. Prevention can be aided by not letting the ground on which the birds run become over used, or by trying to avoid having turkeys and chickens running together in the same pen.

Botulism

This condition affects a bird's control of the neck muscles and is more commonly known as Limber Neck. It is a problem more commonly found in waterfowl than chickens due to the fact that they are more likely to 'shovel' around in the mud, and this is where the bacteria thrives. The principal signs are paralysis of the legs, wings and neck in waterfowl, but in chickens it is more often diarrhoea and ruffled feathers.

Bumblefoot

This is the common name for a common problem which results in inflammation and an occasionally severe swelling on the pad of the foot. It can develop from a cut or graze that heals over, leaving the infection to fester *inside* the skin. This can also be the result of birds perching on rough perches or at too high a height, resulting in bad landings on rough ground, or being allowed onto ground covered with sharp gravel which can break the skin, allowing the bacteria to gain access and infect the foot.

Bumblefoot is actually a bacterial infection and affects the feet of many species of bird – chickens just happen to be very susceptible to it. The condition is often visible as a small red swelling under the base of the foot, together with a black centre spot *inside* the swelling. If the skin breaks the swollen area may bleed, and if opened there will be signs of pus. Birds will often limp and will not rest any weight on the infected foot. If it is left untreated the infection can become very serious and can cause disfigurement of the feet and toes, leading to eventual difficulties in both walking and perching. Birds falling victim to bumblefoot may also exhibit a noticeable increase in temperature too.

In order to reduce the likelihood of bumblefoot, make sure there are no jagged edges or rough perches which might pierce the skin. Perches should be set above the height of the pop-hole

Bumblefoot.

opening but at about 40cm (16inches) above ground and their width should be about 5-7cm (2-3 inches) with rounded edges to improve comfort for the birds when roosting. Also remove any sharp stones from the run, or do not site it on sharp gravel, certainly in the case of larger, heavier birds.

As a bacterial infection bumblefoot can be treated by using antibiotics. Birds with bad infections should be taken to the vet for the feet to be examined, and the vet can then prescribe a course of appropriate antibiotics. The bird's feet should be disinfected, and for this you can use an antibacterial animal spray or a controlled iodine solution. While the foot is healing the bird needs to be kept isolated in a restricted area with clean, soft bedding to avoid further injury or damage to the foot.

You can treat bumblefoot at home, and there are remedies that some people claim help relieve the infection without the need to visit a vet; these include bathing the infected area, disinfecting it and then applying an ointment of either calendula cream or comfrey cream in the morning and evening to cleanse the infection and reduce the swelling. If you feel up to it you can clean the foot with warm salty water, find the pus spot and then lance the swelling with a very sharp knife or scalpel, squeezing out the puss. If possible try to gently remove the head (the black spot) with the scalpel point or cotton buds.

Caecal Worms

These are mentioned in several sections dealing with internal chicken problems. They are a small, whitish parasitic worm that affects poultry and game birds and usually measures up to 1.5cm (¾ inches) in length. They live in the caecum and, although they do not cause disease themselves, they are capable of transmitting blackhead through their eggs. They can be dealt with by using a suitable and readily available wormer.

Chronic Respiratory Disease

This is the chicken equivalent of a cold and, just like with human beings, it is an infection to which chickens are particularly susceptible. In common with us they also exhibit signs of wheezing, sneezing and coughing. The initial cause is usually a viral infection that is followed by a secondary infection, and normally it will clear up quickly if the infection is only a mild one, but if it becomes more severe then it may require the birds being treated with antibiotics.

Coccidiosis

'Cocci', as this problem is usually known, is very common worldwide and is more prevalent during warm, humid weather. It affects the intestinal tract. The symptoms are signs of droopiness, standing huddled up with ruffled feathers and a complete loss of interest in drinking and eating. Growth and weight loss are usually very evident, and quite quickly, together with watery, pasty tan-coloured droppings that are often tinged with blood.

Coccidiosis causes very high losses in flocks across the world and affects mainly chicks and growers whilst in the brooder. The birds tend to pick up the parasite through the droppings of other birds. It is usually spread round the brooder on the birds' feet and invariably ends up on feeders and drinkers. It usually arrives in a flock via wild birds.

Comb and Wattle Damage

The main reasons for damage to combs or wattles is most likely to be an argument with other birds, breeding or a spell of extreme cold weather when these extremities are affected by freezing temperatures. Signs of damage are usually very obvious, with marks, tears or blood in the case of fighting, and black, or very occasionally white marks, a sign of frostbite, although they can at times be related to other ailments; for this reason affected birds should be monitored and further advice sought. In the case of sudden cold spells rubbing in a generous amount of Vaseline will protect the vulnerable parts, and antibiotics will

A young bird suffering from coccidiosis.

A 30 week old bird with Coryza.

help to avoid infection where injury has already occurred.

Coryza

This is a chronic highly infectious disease that affects chickens, and also affects pheasants and guinea fowl. Signs of inflammation of the upper respiratory tract (the side of the face/nose), nasal discharge, facial swelling and a loss of appetite are the usual signs, and in serious cases antibiotic treatment may be required.

Crop Bound

Also known as crop impaction, this is not a disease but rather a condition. The normal cause is that a bird has eaten feathers, long grass or even litter left lying around, creating a blockage, and due to this blockage feed becomes stuck in the crop, not allowing it to pass on into the stomach. The crop will feel hard to the touch and very solid.

Egg Bound (Impaction of the Oviduct)

Again this is a condition, not a disease. Egg bound is when a bird produces an egg but cannot lay it. The symptoms will be behavioural, with the bird

sitting for long periods on the floor, where she will be seen to be straining to try and pass the egg. The vent area may be swollen too, and she could produce very large droppings. This is a potentially very serious internal condition and if not treated quickly it can result in the loss of the bird.

Egg Peritonitis

This is often the result of a bird being egg bound. It is a disorder caused by either a whole or a broken egg being left inside the body. Affected chickens ususally adopt an upright stance, almost like a penguin. This helps to relieve the pressure on the abdomen. The chicken will lose weight but this is not always obvious to the untrained eye. It usually results in the loss of the bird.

Egg Drop Syndrome (EDS)

This is an infectious disease caused by a virus. It most often results in otherwise healthy birds laying thin or soft-shelled eggs. Traditionally it was associated more with ducks and geese but it has become a serious problem with chickens too, especially commercial broilers and layers. The virus is spread through the birds' droppings, so hygiene is very important.

Fowl Cholera

This affects the respiratory system and the principal signs are a cheesy nasal discharge, loss of weight, increasingly thirsty birds, lameness and swelling in the legs, wing joints, foot pads and wattles. Sinuses often become swollen too, and the eyes sticky. Affected birds will also encounter breathing difficulties combined with a rattling sound in the throat and sneezing.

Fowl Pox

This is also referred to as avian pox or chicken pox but has nothing to do with the human 'chicken pox' often found in young children. It affects a bird's skin and spreads quite slowly, usually lasting between three and five weeks. The symptoms are clear or whitish warts on the comb which then turn yellowish, eventually becoming reddish brown or black scabs that bleed. These scabs will eventually fall off, leaving scars. Sometimes these scabs can affect the eyelids, vent area, feet and legs, and there can also be restricted growth and even weight loss. Fowl pox is sometimes mistakenly thought to be 'canker'.

Gapeworms

Birds that can be seen opening their mouths and 'gaping' without making any sound may be infected by gapeworms. The infection is caused by the worm *Syngamus trachea* blocking the windpipe. These worms are usually picked up from the soil or feed and travel through to the lungs and trachea, where they become embedded. In addition to breathing difficulties a bird will also encounter difficulty eating and breeding, and the beak will usually be permanently open. Affected birds should be isolated. Keeping the ground clean and regularly moving runs is the best way of preventing this problem.

Gumboro Disease

Also known as Infectious Bursal Disease (IBD), this is a viral disease that affects young chicks. It attacks an important organ vital to the development of a young chick's immune system. The virus is very resilient but can be killed by most approved disinfectants. It does, however, spread rapidly through bird-to-bird contact and will survive dormant for long periods on certain objects and in contaminated feed. The signs are a whitish or watery diarrhoea that also contains mucus. Check too for sticky litter in the coop and soiled vent feathers. Affected birds will show signs of droopiness and a loss of appetite, but normally only birds up to about four months old are affected. As with many diseases, cleanliness and hygiene are of the utmost importance in prevention.

A bird suffering from fowl pox.

Hock Burns

This is a condition which usually affects meat birds and broilers, but if you have any birds that refuse to perch then there is a possibility that they may be suffering from this problem. The cause is principally birds sitting on floors or bedding contaminated with droppings that produce ammonia – you will often recognise the distinctive smell when you come to clean out a coop. This seems to affect the birds through burns, and in some cases blisters, on the hocks and legs. Prevention is a management issue best achieved by making sure the birds are housed in a correct manner with litter replaced regularly and the use of a good disinfectant such as BioDri.

Infectious Bronchitis (IB)

IB is common across the whole world and affects the respiratory system. It can begin very suddenly and spreads very rapidly throughout a flock, taking only between twenty four and forty eight hours to affect *all* the birds. The symptoms for birds of *all* ages include gasping, coughing, sneezing, rattling (in the breathing), wet eyes and a nasal discharge. Whenever encountered, as it spreads so rapidly, it will usually affect *all* the birds. An outbreak is sometimes wrongly diagnosed as *Laryngotracheitis* or Newcastle disease, but both of these spread more slowly than IB, and are far more severe.

Laryngotracheitis

Often referred to as LT, laryngo, ILT or avian *diphtheria*, this is a really acute disease that spreads quite slowly. It can and often does affect an entire flock, and affected birds will either die or recover within two weeks. The symptoms include watery eyes, swollen sinuses, nasal discharge, coughing (which can sometimes produce a bloody mucus that is left on the face and feathers), head shaking, gasping, choking, gurgling, rattling, whistling and a 'cawing' (best described as a sound that seems to be made as birds try to clear their throats).

Signs of infectious laryngotracheitis.

A bird showing severe signs of respiratory disease.

Lice

These are the single most common parasite found on poultry. They are usually found in the areas around the vent, thighs and breast, and by parting the feathers of affected birds they can usually be seen running for cover. Their eggs can be seen in clusters at the base of the feathers and resemble small cotton wool balls. They need to be removed, and this may mean the removal of some of the feathers too, in order to make sure all the egg cases are eradicated. Any affected bird then needs to be treated with a suitable mite spray, making sure the liquid penetrates right down *into* the feather base. Lice are an irritant that can adversely affect a bird's well-being and also their laying ability. A regular treatment regime is critical.

Marek's Disease

Possibly the disease responsible for the death of more chickens across the world than any other single ailment, and so common that many keepers will, at one time or another, encounter its effects. It is a virus that causes paralysis and affects various parts of a chicken's body. The usual symptoms are droopy wings, paralysis of the leg, a head held low, a twisted neck, blindness, and in many cases sudden death. Losses from this disease in any unvaccinated flocks will probably be up to 50% of the birds.

A bird with a very pale comb. This could be due to red mite or possibly just a sign of moulting as the eyes remain bright and alert.

Mites

The term 'mites' covers a wide variety of insects, including red, depluming, forage, northern and scaly leg mites – each one poses a distinctly different problem for the poultry keeper and as such has to be dealt with individually. There are many available products for the treatment of mites, and regular use of these products should keep them under control and at a level at which they are not a nuisance to the birds. Vigilance and a regular regime are essential in combating them. Complacency is the thing they really thrive on.

Red Mite

This is an insect that thrives in and around poultry. They live in chicken sheds and coops, hiding in any cracks and crevices during daylight hours then, as darkness falls, they emerge from their hiding places to feed off the birds by sucking their blood. The symptoms are listlessness, pale combs and wattles, the birds eventually becoming weak in cases of excessive infestation, and in some case not being able to stand. They are a major irritant to poultry, and in extreme cases can have a very serious effect on birds' health. Treatment is to the housing, not the bird, and *must* be constant, ongoing, maintained in every season of the year, and must be repeated on a regular basis. They may be less of a problem in winter but they are ever

present in a coop. Spread by wild bird populations, they will very soon be present even in brand new coops. With regard to red mite there is absolutely no room for complacency.

Northern Mite

These are grey in colour and unlike red mite they live their whole lifecycle *on* the chicken. Again they must be controlled as a matter of flock welfare. They are spread from bird to bird through litter in the housing, often falling off a host bird and then finding a new host very quickly, so the problem can spread rapidly through a flock. Regular treatment at least once every three weeks will help to keep them under control.

Depluming Mite

These live in a bird's plumage, and as their name suggests, this is where they cause damage. Although not that common they do require preventative action using a suitable treatment.

Crest Mite

A dark brown mite associated with exhibition breeds such as the Poland. It lives its whole life on the bird and infestation is rapid. Infested birds will scratch and it can cause permanent damage to their eyes.

Forage Mite

This is a parasite that can be present in large numbers in dirty poultry housing. They are very common in situations where birds are being reared intensively for the table and live in litter and occasionally on dead birds, causing considerable irritation. They are also capable of spreading viral infections, and can become a source of considerable skin irritation for the keepers of affected birds too. A regular hygiene programme should keep them under control and should certainly be the first course of action if ever they are discovered.

Scaly leg mite.

Scaly Leg Mite

After the dreaded red mite, scaly leg mite is probably the second most common of all mite found in poultry, and they affect *all* poultry. Scaly leg mite are hard to detect in the early stages and often go unnoticed, especially where the keeper may be inexperienced, and perhaps spending much of the time seeking out the more often mentioned red mite. Consequently they can often be a serious problem by the time their presence is discovered. There will be visible signs on the scales of the legs, with the first sign being that the scales start to rise very slightly due to mite activity beneath. The problem usually begins on the unfeathered part of the leg and the upper half of the toes. It then spreads and will ultimately affect most of the leg, becoming ever more apparent as the infestation spreads. As the mite bite into the bird's flesh it creates blisters and these lift the scales, causing considerable damage and discomfort as the cycle continues with breeding and egg laying. As the

eggs hatch the infestation worsens, sometimes making the legs look as though they have doubled in thickness, with birds sometimes unable to walk in extreme cases – they may even start to pick off the scales themselves. At this point the situation is life-threatening and will no doubt be a problem throughout the flock as the problem is spread through dirty bedding. The only solution is a major clean out of the housing, when early observation could have prevented or controlled the problem.

To treat the problem wrap the bird in a towel, but not too tightly – just enough to exercise control. You can then confirm just how serious the problem is. Mild cases can be treated with various sprays and by then using a brush to make sure the liquid gets right down into the scales so the mite can be eradicated. Really bad infestations will need a more radical treatment after consulting a vet, who will most likely prescribe Ivomec, a prescription only treatment for mite administered to the back of the neck from where it enters the bloodstream, a little like a dog flea treatment. This will certainly kill the mite, but it usually helps if you have a vet who is familiar with poultry requirements. The scales will eventually fall off then grow back. The old-fashioned method required creosote, diesel and surgical spirit, but these methods are not really acceptable with all today's rules and regulations. After any treatment use a good coating of Vaseline to suffocated any remaining mite. This method is certainly well proven, but don't expect overnight results as it will take quite some time for the legs to heal completely.

Mycoplasma (MG)

This can cause very acute respiratory problems similar to *Coryza, Sinusitis* and Bronchitis. It is very contagious and will spread quickly through a flock, affecting birds of all ages, and after an outbreak any remaining birds can become carriers of the disease without showing any outward signs. The disease is diagnosed by a blood test, and if found requires immediate treatment and control.

Signs of MG include gurgling and sneezing as the

lungs become affected. Birds will look ill and stand with feathers fluffed out and eyes closed. Many birds will not recover from an outbreak within the flock as mortality rates are typically high.

Newcastle Disease

Also known as avian distemper or fowl pest, this is another well known worldwide disease. It affects both the respiratory and nervous systems of birds. An outbreak can occur very suddenly and the disease can take hold of an entire flock within just a week. As with other respiratory type diseases the symptoms are primarily wheezing, coughing and chirping, followed by nervous disorders such as drooping wings and a twisted neck. The percentage of a flock affected will be very high as the disease is extremely contagious and spreads very easily from bird to bird.

Poisoning

Although it may sometimes seem to the frustrated chicken keeper as if their birds can eat just about anything, there are actually many compounds that are toxic to them, including some plants, disinfectants and pesticides. I have included a list of these in Chapter 4, Making Sure Your Healthy Hens Have A Healthy Environment. For the most part chickens are generally careful what they eat, but checking the area in which they run for any potential risks can avert a potential threat to your birds.

Pullorum

This serous disease was originally known as Bacillary White Diarrhoea, and Salmonellosis pullorum is its cause. It is primarily a disease of young chicks and turkey poults, and is spread to the young via the egg or by other infected chicks, normally in the hatchery. The symptoms are mainly seen in very young chicks less than 3 weeks old, but it often only becomes apparent as a result of high numbers of chicks dying either in shell or very soon after hatching. Diagnosis is difficult, with the

only signs being white diarrhoea and pasting of the vent. Treatment with antibiotics is possible but is not recommended as affected birds will become carriers and create considerable devastation later.

Rickets

As with young children many years ago, this condition involves the softening of the bones in young birds. It can be prevented by giving birds the correct levels of calcium, phosphorus and vitamin D. The condition is now very rare due to today's comprehensive feed additives and the research done by feed manufacturers to provide complete diets for all types of poultry.

Roundworm

Most birds have a small amount of roundworm which can be endured up to a certain level, but if left uncontrolled and in unhygienic conditions these worms can increase at an alarming rate. The results are worms about 5cm in length which are found in the bird's gut. The symptoms are usually anaemia and eggs with very pale yolks. Keep your birds in clean conditions and make sure the ground on which they forage is kept fresh and treated, especially if they are restricted to a fixed run. If possible re-site the run regularly to provide them with uncontaminated ground.

Salmonellosis

All species of bird, and all ages, are susceptible to this chronic disease. There is evidence that 75% of all chickens are infected with some kind of salmonellae at some times in their lives, and saying this publicly got Edwina Currie into considerable trouble many years ago. This bacteria is a very serious problem for poultry keepers due to the fact that chickens will appear perfectly healthy, but can be carriers. The causes of an outbreak among a flock can include stress, overcrowding, moulting, medical treatment and lack of feed, but transmission itself is normally either through the egg or by faecal contamination of feed, water, the incubation process, exploding eggs (usually due to expanding gases in a rotten egg), or bird to bird.

Salmonellosis is now regarded as having been eradicated from most commercial flocks, but there are still occasional outbreaks, especially in commercial flocks in Third World countries. The symptoms are young birds with pasted vents and white diarrhoea, often hunched up and appearing sleepy together with lameness, blindness and showing signs of laboured breathing. Mortality usually peaks at about seven to ten days, and can be as high as 100 percent. Adult birds are usually affected sub-clinically, with effects ranging from a drop in egg production and fertility to hatchability of eggs. Depression, anorexia, diarrhoea and dehydration are also occasionally seen.

There are actually some 2500 recognised different strains of salmonella, and although they rarely cause disease they can affect humans through the consumption of a diverse range of food products, including eggs. The effects, although unpleasant, are usually short-lived.

Swollen Hocks

This is a condition generally found in broiler chickens and also in turkeys raised for meat. The problem is associated with birds roosting on the floor on poor, dirty litter that contains high levels of ammonia. Although the cause is not totally clear it is understood that the ammonia from the droppings in the litter causes the infection and the swelling. There is no actual treatment but keeping the litter clean and dry and using a suitable powder disinfectant such as BioDri will help to prevent the problem occurring.

Stress

Stress is a major factor which can undermine the general health and well-being of your birds. It can come in many forms and seems to affect them in different ways, but it is particularly common in show birds. It seems as though pure breeds are more susceptible due to their genetic makeup, and birds with the best colours and best types always seem to have the worst reactions to stress. We have all heard tales of crossbred pedigree dogs, with the 'mutt' always seeming to be in good health while the pedigree breed almost has built-in problems. The same seems to be true with the breeding of fancy fowl too. The finer the breed, the more susceptible they seem to stress and disease.

By nature, most chickens (and waterfowl too) are quite cowardly, and sometimes seem to be afraid of their own shadows. Chickens have an in-built 'flight' instinct, and even the hand-reared and tame ones still tend to panic. It is usually this in-built fear that seems to cause stress. If anything out of the ordinary or unexpected occurs, a panic gene seems to be triggered. Ultimately, in more extreme cases of stress, the experience can cause a physical reaction, enabling disease to take hold of what may otherwise be a perfectly healthy bird.

Without going into too much poultry veterinary detail, stress causes changes that occur in the gut which lower the pH level, and when the pH level is low the 'gram negative' bacteria find the environment more accommodating, take hold and replicate at a much greater rate, and from this a variety of problems and diseases can occur.

Stress in chickens can be caused by changes in temperature, extremes of weather, changes in feeding routines, nutrition, handling (and certainly excessive handling), changes in housing, introducing new birds (or removing familiar ones), noise, chaos, boisterous children, an unfamiliar dog, a bird of prey – in fact just about anything they might be uncertain about or unfamiliar with. *All* birds have their own expectations of what is normal, and anything outside of this comfort zone can result in raised levels of stress. Show birds, in addition, require preparation, bathing, grooming, clipping and being transported from A to B – none of them normal everyday experiences for birds, especially those unfamiliar with it. It would be impossible to cover all aspects of this complex area, but you probably get the general idea.

Twisted and deformed toes.

Tapeworms

The term 'tapeworm' covers a number of different species ranging from a microscopic size up to thirteen inches in length. It is estimated that over 50 per cent of all chickens have some infestation from these worms. The worm lodges itself to the intestinal tract and attaches its head by means of four pairs of suckers, and each species prefers to infest a different section of the intestine. The symptoms of infestation include dull feathers, slow movement, weight loss, respiratory problems, paralysis and eventually death in extreme cases of infestation or if left untreated. Tapeworms require an intermediate host such as a beetle, earthworm, fly, slug, snail or termite and chickens then pick up the infection by eating the insect or other worm carrier. The worms produce huge quantities of eggs so the infestation increases at a rapid rate. To control tapeworms you must first control the hosts, and keeping insect numbers to a minimum and the coop clean will help to prevent these worms from infecting your birds.

Twisted Leg (Crooked Leg)

This is quite a common problem in broiler birds. The bones in the legs are affected and the problem usually appears very suddenly. The symptoms are that one or both the legs bend outwards to such a degree that the birds will sometimes walk on swollen hocks; this can take effect from as early as one week onwards. The cause is not really understood but could possibly be due to a slipped tendon. Prevention is usually by rearing the birds on clean litter and reducing the amount of fast growth feed, as growing too quickly will make the problem considerably worse. There is no actual cure for the condition.

Twisted Toes

Usually affecting very young chicks, twisted toes – also called crooked or deformed toes – is usually the result of breeding problems or incorrect temperatures in the incubator or during the very early stages of the brooding process. The toes curl either to the the left or the right, resulting in the young chick walking on the sides of the toes. There is no cure but setting the incubator correctly should reduce the occurrence. Birds with twisted toes can often enjoy a reasonable life.

Vent Gleet (Pasted Vent)

This is common in chicks and, as the name implies, affects the vent area, with chicks up to ten days old showing signs of droopiness and with sticky droppings giving off a very bad odour. The cause is usually either incorrect feeding or chicks becoming chilled during the incubation or brooding period. It is not an infectious problem and can be avoided by keeping chicks warm and ensuring that they have appropriate feed. Under no circumstances should you breed from a hen that has previously suffered from this complaint. It is usually a kindness to cull any chicks that do not recover.

DIAGNOSTIC GUIDE TO POULTRY AILMENTS AND TREATMENT		
HEAD AND NECK		
SIGNS OF DISEASE	CAUSES	TREATMENT/PREVENTION
Crossed beak, top beak overgrown	Genetic, nutritional	Might be an inherited defect. Trim to shape Check diet
Listless, eyes dull and lifeless	Part of any general disease	Check for other symptoms
Eye discharge, one eye or both	Local infection as a result of dust or environmental factors/bacterial infection. Part of generalized infection such as *Mycoplamosis*. Look for other symptoms	Bathe the eye with saline solution and treat with antibiotic eye drops or cream. If *Mycoplasmosis* treat with a soluble antibiotic such as Tylosin
Eyes Sunk into Sockets	Dehydration usually due to diarrhoea. Need to determine the cause of the diarrhoea	Make sure a plentiful supply of clean drinking water is available until a diagnosis is made
Comb and wattle pale and looking anaemic	May just be immaturity if youngster and comb small	
	External parasites (red mite, lice)	Treat for red mite and lice. Spray house
	Internal parasites	Anthelmintic in the feed usually for up to 7 days
White scabs and flakey	Scaly face of Favus. Fungal infection. *Microsporum gallinae*	Use gloves and rub in athlete's foot cream for 7 days. Avoid eyes. Treat premises with Virkon or F10
Purple comb when normally red	Heat failure due to age/weight	Individual treatment possible. See vet
	Nitrate poisoning	Methylene blue in water
	Severe respiratory distress	Needs further diagnosis
Nasel discharge with sneezing	Dusty environment	Imrove ventilation and get rid of dust
	Probably general infection such as *Mycoplasmosis*. Needs further diagnosis	Soluable antibiotic in the drinking water, depending on the cause
Swollen sinus(es)	Part of general infection/*Mycoplasmosis*	Soluable antibiotic, depending on the cause
Ears: cheese like substance in ear canal	Bacterial or mite infection	Olive oil drops (not licensed for use), dog ear drops - need to consult vet
Cheese-like material in mouth and back of throat	Canker due to *Trichomonas infection*	Metronidazole in water. Vitamin supplement
SKIN AND FEATHERS		
SIGNS	CAUSES	TREATMENT/PREVENTION
Losing feathers	Normal moult. Usually 3-4 weeks in late summer/early autumn	Check nutritian. May need supplement if prolonged
Feather pecking often with vent pecking	May be a sign of bullying. May cause bleeding and death if not stopped. Overcrowding and stress can be factors	Isolate culprit. Usually the bird with all its feathers remaining. Check environment. Treat wounds with antibiotic spray
Losing feathers and itchy	External parasites: red mite, lice	Powder over birds and perches. Treat house
Raised, crusty lesions on legs. Scaly Leg	Skin mites	Dunk legs in surgical spirit weekly

The Healthy Hens Handbook

SKIN AND FEATHERS CONTINUED		
SIGNS	CAUSES	TREATMENT / PREVENTION
Nasty smell with scabby, inflamed vent with yellow discharge	Vent Gleet as a result of Herpes virus infection	Cider Apple Vinegar in water. Keep coop and surroundings clean. Apply anti-fungal cream
Spoiling arouind the vent or pasted around the vent	Any form of diarrhoea	Diagnosis required for treatment
Pendulous crop	Crop bound usually due to poor, over fibrous diet. Usually older birds	Isolate and starve with water for 38 hours. May require surgery in extreme cases
Swollen crop with sour smell, bird lethargic	Sour crop due to yeast infection	

BREATHING		
SIGNS	CAUSES	TREATMENT/PREVENTION
Rapid breathing with eye and nasel discharge and swollen sinuses	*Mycoplasmosis*	Soluble antibiotic such as Tylosin. Disinfect premises
Increased breathing rate, often with reduced egg quality (wrinkled shells)	Infectious bronchitis due to corona virus infection. High mortality possible in the young	No treatment. Vaccination is effective as prevention. Adults may be carriers
Breathing distress with gasping and death	*Aspergillosis* - fungal infection like 'Farmers Lung' affecting mostly young poulty and can infect people	Cull affected birds, treat environment. Get rid of damp litter
Large numbers of birds gasping, sick and dying with eye and nasal discharge, comb and wattle often very dark	Avian (bird) flu. Several viruses, varing pathogenicity. Highly infectious. NB Notifiable disease and possibly infectious to people	Blood test required to confirm
Gasping or gaping breathing with diarrhoea	Gape worms. *Syngamus trachea*	Anthelmintic daily in the feed for 7 days - Flubendazole. Eggs must not be consumed for 7 days from the end of treatment. Same for meat.

DIARRHOEA		
SIGNS	CAUSES	TREATMENT/PREVENTION
Diarrhoea white in colour with perhaps some blood. Young birds over 21 days old	*Coccidiosis*, usually *Eimeria* species	Coddidiostats. Make sure litter is dry. To prevent put coccidiostat in feed
White diarrhoea - often fatal in young birds	*Salmonella pullorum*. Needs bacteriology and blood tests to diagnose. *Salmonella typhinurium/enteritidis* - NB Notifiable disease with potential to infect people	Antibiotic - see vet. Cull adult carriers. Clean up environment. Vaccination is possible
Yellow diarrhoea, mostly turkeys and pheasants. Uncommon in chickens, Can be high mortality in turkeys and pheasants.	Blackhead caused by *protozoe*. *Histomonas* parasite carried by intestinal worm *Heterakis gallinarum*. Mostly affects turkeys, but *Heterakis* worm is carried by chickens	Treat with metronidazole in water for 5 days. Worm hens to get rid of intermediate host, Heterakis. Never keep chickens and turkeys together
Green diarrhoea along with respiratory and nervous system	Newcatle disease/Fowl pest due to paramyxovirus infection. NB Notifiable disease	UK is mostly clear of disease. Recommend only to vaccinate in face of outbreak

DIARRHOEA		
SIGNS	CAUSES	TREATMENT / PREVENTION
Green colour diarrhoea	Too much green food, especiall cabbage	Check diet
Green colour diarrhoea and listless	Intestinal parasitic worms	Flubendazole in feed for 7 days. Should treat twice a year. Eggs and meat cannot be consumed for 7 days after treatment. Clean environment
Brown Diarrhoea in young birds from about 5 days old	E.coli infection. Stress factors/cold and dirty wet litter	Soluble antibiotic in water for up to a week. *Oxytetracycline* and *apramycin*. Improve environment

LAMENESS		
SIGNS	CAUSES	TREATMENT / PREVENTION
Swelling on foot, mostly underside	Bumblefoot, usually bacterial infection in older, heavy birds	Antibiotic and poulticing. May need surgery. Guarded outlook for recover
Paralysis, same side wing and leg	Mareks disease due to a Herpes virus. Various strains	Cull affected birds. No effective treatment. Vaccinate. Keep youngsters away from possible adult carriers
Non-specifc lameness	Injury or tumour or arthritis. Kidney disease	Needs more diagnosis before treatment. If injury and not fracture then complete rest will be indicated
	Potential fracture	Would need vet input. Many simple fractures can be splinted
	Perosis due to bird growing too rapidly to allow sufficient calcium and phosphorus in the bones	Check nutrition/reduce protein in diet. Check vitamin and mineral content of the diet
	Lameness in one or both legs may be due to internal parasites	Check faeces for parasite eggs and treat with Flubendazole in feed for 7 days, if positive
Swollen hocks	Arthritis or *Mycoplasma* infection	Antibiotic such as *Tylosin* or *Lincolycin* if infection diagnosed. For non-infective causes use non-steroidal anti-inflammatory drugs eg. Meloxican. NB Not licensed and need to see vet
	In young birds deformation of bones and joints may indicate metabolic disease due to calcium/phosphorus imbalance in diet.	Check diet with vet and rectify if necessary
Splay Legs	Common problem in newly hached. Could be nutritional or slippery surface	Tie legs together with soft wool for 2-3 days, but not usually successful and would need to cull
Deformities	Common inherited deformities. Roach back (*Kyphosis*), *Scoliosis*, Cow hocks, inwardly bent toes	Most birds with severe deformities should be culled

The Healthy Hens Handbook

BEHAVIOUR		
SIGNS OF DISEASE	CAUSES	TREATMENT/PREVENTION
Weight loss but still bright and feeding	Nutritional ie inadequate diet	Check diet
	Intestinal worms	Flubendazole daily in food for 7 days
	Avian Tuberculosis (NB potential to infect people	Not treatment. Cull affected birds
Any change in flock or individual behaviour	May be stress related	Dim lights if possible. Shut in shed for a time if possible. Apply vitamins and probiotics

ADULT SUDDEN DEATH		
SIGNS OF DISEASE	CAUSES	TREATMENT/PREVENTION
Without prior warning	Need for post-mortem. Consider predator eg. fox, mink etc. Egg Peritonitis, Result of yolk in abdomen missing oviduct, Heart failure Kidney failure, *Aspergillosis* Botulism, Newcastle disease (Notifiable disease)	Probable more common causes of sudden death
	Poisoning: blue green algae.	Keep water containers clean. Stop access to stagnant water
	Plant poisoning or chemical poisons eg arsenic, lead, slug bait, pesticides	Check for and remove laburnum seeds, potato sprouts, black nightshade, hanbane, iris, privet, rhododendron, yew, caster oil, sweet pea, rapeseed, clematis, St John's wort, vetch, ragwort, rhubarb leaves and some fungi

YOUNG SUDDEN DEATH		
SIGNS OF DISEASE	CAUSES	TREATMENT / PREVENTION
Without prior warning	Consider predator eg. fox.	Poor enironment - too hot or cold
	Smothering	Not enough space. Excessive crowding
	Gumboro disease (infectious Bursitis	Vaccinate breeding birds, can protect chicks
	Salmonellosis	
	Newcastle disease	

EGG LAYING		
SIGNS	CAUSES	TREATMENT / PREVENTION
Laying adult birds - no eggs	Fright or stress (new home?)	Make nest box darker?
	Laying out of next box	Check for redmite
No eggs, listless and straining in adults	Egg bound. Remove if possible but this can lead to prolapse	Possible need of a vet. Cull if egg peritonitis
Prolapsed vent/oviduct	Often found dead due to pecking by companions. Age, stress, being overweight or laying too young can all be precipitating factors	A cure is often possible with lots of patience and TLC (see page 103). Surgery is usually not a viable option

This table was first produced in The Smallholder's Guide to Animal Ailments by Russell Lyon BVM&S, MRCVS.

A GLOSSARY OF TERMS

Abdomen: the area under the body from rear to breast.

Abscess: pus filled area.

Addled eggs: eggs that were fertile but have died during incubation.

Air cell: area inside the egg that contains oxygen (at the wide end)

Albumen: the white protein area of the egg.

Alektorophobia: fear of poultry (chickens)

Alimentary tract: the tube where the digestion and egestion take place – this runs from the mouth to the vent.

Allantois: this is the sac that is connected to the abdomen of the embryo, allowing it to breathe.

Amino acids: digested proteins ready for absorption into the bloodstream.

Amnion: this is a transparent sac filled with fluid that surrounds the embryo.

Anaemia: a blood deficiency that causes weakness and pale skin.

Antibiotics: medicines used for the treatment of bacterial infections.

Antibodies: agents that are in the bone marrow, spleen and blood that are circulated as a defence against viral disease.

Ark: chicken housing in various shapes and sizes, and generally movable.

AI (artificial insemination): a way of fertilizing by putting semen through a syringe into the oviduct of the female.

Ash: an ingredient of poultry feed.

Atrophy: a condition that describes the shrinking or wasting away of part of the body.

Avian: relating to birds.

A bird with anaemia.

Autosexing. Left = female, right = male. Note paler colour in the male.

Bearded Silkie.

Autosexing breeds: chickens that are bred to provide easily identifiable chicks at a day old.

Axial feather: small feather between the primary and secondary feathers.

Bantam: a small chicken that is a miniature version of the equivalent in large fowl.

Barring: the pattern or arrangement of different coloured stripes in feathers.

Battery system: a commercial intensive system of egg production usually in cages, although barn production is the more modern and acceptable method.

Beak: the mouth of the bird, consisting of upper and lower mandible.

Beak trimming: removing a small section of the upper part of the beak to prevent cannibalism and feather pecking.

Beard: tufted feathers under the beak which are present on certain breeds.

Bedding: material on the floor of a coop to absorb moisture, droppings etc., normally shavings or straw.

Blade: describes the lower part of a straight comb on a bird's head.

Bleaching: loss of colour in plumage and other parts of a bird's body, in some cases caused by the birds being outside.

Blood spot: red spot in a freshly laid egg.

Blowout: another description of a prolapse, a problem caused in most cases by laying too large an egg.

Booted: feathered legs on chickens.

Breast: the part of the chicken's body from the neck through the central part of the body down to between the legs.

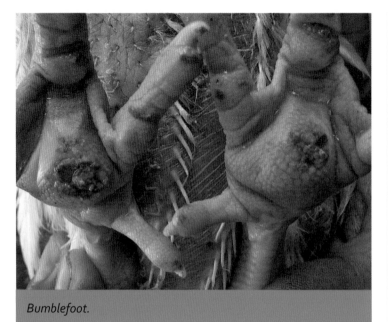

Bumblefoot.

Checking for mites.

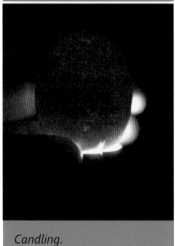

Candling.

Breed: the description of the various different chicken types available, with different characteristics, colours and sizes defining each individual breed.

Broiler: a chicken reared solely for the table.

Brood: a batch of young chicks.

Brooder: usually an area where the chicks are reared, whether it be natural or by artificial heat.

Brooding period: the time it takes to rear the chicks from a day old until they can be left on their own.

Broody hen: when a chicken becomes broody and lays and sits on her own eggs, or anyone else's if she feels the need.

Candling: Looking through the shell with a light to check the fertility of eggs.

Cannibalism: a very nasty habit that causes chickens to peck and eat other birds with occasionally very serious results.

Cape: feathers between the shoulders and under the hackle.

Carbohydrates: these supply heat and energy and are found in a variety of foods, including grain and vegetables.

Carriage: this describes the way a bird stands and carries itself.

Chalazae: the membrane that keeps a yolk suspended in the middle of an egg.

Chick: a young bird up to the age of approximately 6 to 8 weeks.

Chick crumbs: a starter feed for very young chicks.

Chick's tooth: a very small pointed section on the point of the beak of a chick, and used to pierce and break through the shell.

Clavicle: the wishbone.

Clean-legged: legs showing no feathers.

Clears: infertile eggs showing no sign of development during incubation.

Cloaca: the opening at the end of the rectum.

Close feathering: plumage that is held tightly to the body.

Clutch: the number of eggs laid by a single hen.

Cock: a male chicken over the age of 12 months.

Cockerel: a male chicken under the age of 12 months.

Comb: fleshy addition that sits on top of a bird's head – these come in a variety of shapes and sizes.

Glossary of Terms

Condition: the general state of health and appearance of a bird.

Coop: chicken housing that comes in various forms.

Coverts: small feathers at the base of the tail; the ones on the wings are covering the tops of the flight feathers.

Crest: feather's on top of the head.

Crop: where the food is stored before being passed on into the gizzard for digestion.

Cuckoo: a feather marking very similar to barred.

Culling: disposing of excess, unwanted birds or sick birds.

Cushion: description of the soft feathers on the rump of certain breeds.

Cuticle: the bloom left on an egg as it dries soon after laying.

Day olds: chicks that have just hatched.

Dead-in-shell: embryos that began to develop in the shell but died before hatching.

De-beaking: removal of the top portion of the beak to prevent cannibalism.

Deep litter: a system where the birds are on a deep layer of shavings that are left untouched.

Fowl pox.

Down: soft feathers on a newly hatched chick.

Droppings: a bird's faeces.

Dual purpose: a bird suitable for the production of both meat and eggs.

Dub: surgically removing the comb and wattles from a bird.

Dust bath: a dry area where the birds roll and throw soil and dust through their feathers to help clear away parasites.

Earlobes: bare skin just below the ears.

Ectoparasites: mite, ticks and any other external parasites.

Egg grading: checking eggs for weight and size, ready for human consumption.

Egg wash: a solution that sanitises eggs, whether for eating or incubation.

Embryo: the developing chick inside the shell.

Endoparasites: internal parasites including coccidia and other worms.

Fancier: a person who breeds and owns chickens as a hobby or for exhibition.

Feather legged: legs with feathers.

Fibre: a food element that enables the bowels to work efficiently.

First-cross: the young from the first mating of two different breeds.

Flights: the long wing feathers (also known as the primaries).

Flock: a group of birds living together.

Free range: birds kept outside and allowed to wander and forage.

Frizzle: feathers curled forwards towards a bird's head – several different breeds have this unique feather type.

Fowl pox: also referred to as avian pox or chicken pox. It affects a bird's skin and spreads quite slowly, usually lasting between three and five weeks.

Frizzle.

Gallus domesticus: the Latin name for the domestic chicken.

Gallus gallus: the Latin name for the original chicken or 'red jungle fowl'.

Game birds: a category encompassing several different bird species — with chickens these are hard feathered breeds i.e. Old English Game.

Gapes: when a bird opens and closes its beak as if gasping for breath.

Gizzard: a bird's stomach.

Grower: a bird older than 6 to 8 weeks and being reared to adulthood.

Growers' ration: feed for maturing young birds.

Gullet: the tubular section leading to the entrance of the stomach.

Hackles: narrow, long neck feathers.

Handling: the correct way of catching, picking up and holding a bird.

Hard feathered: the close, tight feathering normally associated with game chickens or Asian poultry breeds.

Hatching: the period during which a chick emerges from the shell.

Heavy breeds: larger breeds that come in different varieties.

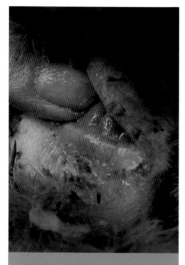

Checking the vent.

Swollen hocks.

Hard feathered – an Asil cockerel.

Hen: a female chicken over 12 months of age.

Humidity: the level of moisture in the air — very important with regard to incubation and hatching.

Hybrid: mainly commercial birds bred from pure breeds for the efficient production of eggs or meat.

Impaction: a blockage in the body, usually in the crop or cloaca.

In-breeding: using related birds in the breeding pen.

Incubation: the process of hatching chickens either by artificial or natural methods.

Incubator: a machine used for artificial hatching.

Infertile: eggs that are not fertile or have not been fertilized.

Joule: a measurement of energy levels in poultry and other animal feeds.

Jejunum: a small middle intestine.

Keel: breast bone.

Kibbling: grain being chopped into small pieces ready for grinding.

Lacing: a feather pattern with the outer edge being, in most cases, a different shade from the rest of the feather.

Layer: an adult hen in full egg production.

Layers' ration/pellets/mash: feed for mature chickens containing all the requirements for birds in lay.

Leader: a term describing the spike end or point at the rear of the comb on certain breeds of chicken.

Leaf comb: a comb that has an appearance similar to a leaf.

Leg feathering: feathers found on the legs of certain breeds which are a requirement of the breed standard.

Light breed: chickens that are light in weight and in most cases more agile.

Litter: the term used to describe bedding and the floor covering in chicken housing.

Maize: a grain ideal as an extra additive or treat which helps to create heat for the bird's bodies in winter.

Mandible: lower part of a bird's beak.

Marbling: spotted pattern on the plumage.

Mash: ground chicken feed containing grains and other ingredients.

Meat spot: a very small speck in the contents of a freshly laid egg.

Mossy-feathered: white feathers spotted with brown.

Mottling: feathers with white tips at the ends – desirable on certain breeds but not on others.

Moulting: a natural annual process of losing and replacing feathers.

Muff: feathers that grow on either side of the face and look a bit like whiskers.

Natural brooding: chicks reared by the mother hen.

Nest: a place for a bird to lay her eggs or hatch chicks.

Nostrils: the openings at the rear of the beak for breathing.

Oats: a grain used in poultry feed.

Oesophagus: area in the digestive system or gullet between the mouth and crop.

Out-breeding: using a different strain of birds of the same breed for breeding.

Oviduct: the passage from the ovary down to the vent where the egg travels to be laid.

Oyster shell: material crushed and used as an additive to feed to provide a source of calcium.

Papilla: part of the shank that eventually develops into a spur as a male bird matures.

Parson's nose: the bony, fleshy part of a bird from which the tail grows, known as the *Uropygium*.

Pasting: a messy vent brought about by loose droppings.

Pathogen: a disease-causing organism.

Pea comb: a small, low comb with a triple section.

Pecking order: a hierarchy decided by the birds as to who is in charge.

Pencilling: markings on the feathers that represent lines.

Perch: a bar (usually wood) on which birds roost and sleep at night.

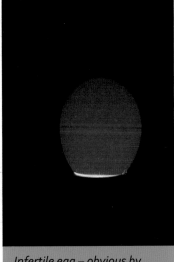

Infertile egg – obvious by candling.

Pin feathers: feathers that are just showing through the skin or have not yet shed the outer covering.

Pipping: the time when a chick is breaking through the shell and a small hole appears.

Pituitary gland: a gland in the brain that controls the egg laying mechanism.

Plumage: the full set of feathers.

Point of lay (POL): the period when a chicken is just reaching maturity and is about to lay for the first time.

Popeye: a condition giving rise to sick and emaciated birds, causing the eyes to look very large.

Pop-hole: the entrance and exit from the poultry housing.

Pot egg: a false egg sometimes made of pot placed in the nest to encourage birds to lay.

Poussin: a bird killed at a young age for the table.

Precocity: birds starting to lay early.

Proventriculus: a glandular stomach area just before the gizzard.

Moulting.

Pullet: female bird under 12 months old.

Pure bred: birds bred from pure bloodstock to keep bloodlines pure.

Rattle: the sound made by a bird when it has a respiratory problem.

Roost: the area a bird uses to sleep at night, normally on a perch.

Rooster: a male bird over the age of one year.

Saddle: the part of a bird's back just before the tail.

Saddle (protector): cover fitted onto a female bird's back during the breeding period to prevent a cockerel damaging a hen.

Scales: the small overlapping plates on a bird's legs and toes.

Secondaries: inner quill feathers on the wings.

Self-colour: birds with a single colour plumage.

Serrations: the divisions/points in the comb.

Setting: putting selected eggs into the incubator.

Setting the incubator.

Trio – one male and two females.

Sex link: birds bred using chromosomes from both parents to enable chicks to be sexed at hatching.

Shank: the area between the foot and the hock joint.

Sheen: the shine on the plumage.

Shell: the outer casing of an egg.

Sickles: long curved tail feathers.

Single comb: narrow, normally quite thin comb with serrations.

Sitting: term describing a set of fertile eggs sold for incubation.

Spangling: a pattern on the plumage with splashes of different colours.

Split comb: where the comb divides but should be single.

Split crest: a division in a bird's crest.

Split tail: a gap in the base of the tail feathers that should not be there.

Spraddle legs: the spread legs of young chicks which prevent them from standing.

Spur: hard, pointed growth on the back of a cock's legs, generally used for fighting.

Strain: a group of birds that have proven breeding from the same family group.

Striping: a dark line down the centre of the feather.

Supplements: vitamins and additives usually given in feed and water.

Swollen hocks: usually found in broiler chickens and turkeys raised for meat. It is associated with dirty litter containing high levels of ammonia.

Thighs: the area of muscle above the shank covered in feathers.

Ticking: small, usually dark dots on the feathers of a show bird and regarded as a fault.

Tipping: tips of feathers which are a different colour to the rest of the feather.

Torticollis: twisted or wry neck.
Toxin: poison produced by micro-organisms.

Trachea: windpipe.

Trap-nest: a special nest box that closes when a bird enters to allow the breeder to identify who is producing which eggs.

Treading: the act of mating when a cock or cockerel mounts the hen.

Tri-coloured: breeds with several different colours on the saddle, hackle and wings.

Trio: a term describing one male and two female chickens.

Twisted leg: This is quite a common problem in broiler birds.

Twisted toes: usually a result of breeding problems or incorrect incubator temperatures.

Utility chickens: birds bred solely for egg or meat production.

Vector: a carrier of disease organisms from one place to another in its own body e.g. ticks, flies and mosquitoes.

Vent: the opening of the oviduct from where an egg is laid.

Ventriculus: another name for the gizzard.

Wind egg (on right) comparred to 'normal' sized egg.

Wind egg showing no yolk formed.

Xanthophylls: pigments found in plants and grasses etc. that can produce darker yolks in eggs if eaten by the birds.

Yolk: – the yellow of an egg that provides the food source for the developing chick.

Yolk sac: the follicle where the ovum and yolk are held until the yolk matures and is released.

Zoonosis: a disease that can be passed from poultry (or any non-human species) to humans.

Vulture hock: feathers that grow out from the leg/hock.

Walnut comb: a type of comb also referred to as a strawberry comb.

Wattles: the lobes suspended from below a bird's jaw.

Weathering: a term describing a white bird's plumage after exposure to sun and weather that has given the feathers a brassy or yellow tinge, also known as 'sappy'.

Web: the areas of skin between the toes and the joints in the wings.

Wheat: a grain feed.

Wind egg: a small egg containing no yolk. Also called 'fairy', 'fart', or 'tiny' eggs.

Wing bay: secondary wing feathers that form a triangular pattern when the wings are folded.

Wing clipping: trimming the ends of a wing to prevent a bird from flying.

Wry tail: a deformity where the tail is twisted to one side.

Warfarin: a poison used on rats, and an anti-coagulant.

The Hen's M.O.T.

To keep birds in top condition they require a regular check up to make sure they are in good health. This is just a basic once over check on top of the everyday visual checks that should be made when letting the birds out in the morning and locking them up for roosting in the evening. Picking the bird up and looking closely at the head, body and feet should inform you of any problems, and a healthy bird will certainly be keen to rejoin the flock. Look for pests, swellings (particularly on the feet), runny eyes or nose and a clear vent. This regular check could save a lot of trouble in the long run.

> The ideal time of year for your MOT is in autumn when you are preparing your birds for the long winter snap.

Combs and Wattles

A general health care regime is essential all year round, and we check our birds every day to make sure they are in good condition. In the autumn, however, it is a good idea to be a bit more thorough and really look in detail at the condition of the legs, feet, comb, wattles and eyes. Checking birds in really bad weather can be difficult, especially if you work and the daylight hours are limited.

There are spells when the temperature reaches well below freezing. This is the time to make sure the comb and wattles are protected by simply rubbing in some Vaseline. This will protect them from the damage that the freezing weather can inflict. If left untreated, the comb and wattles can freeze and turn black, and although this is not life-threatening, it must be very uncomfortable.

Treating scaly leg with a spray.

Feet and Legs

Feet and legs need to be checked to make sure there are no mite present. If any of the scales on the legs are showing signs of rising, then you may have a problem with leg mite. This will need to be treated as soon as possible, as it does spread, and during the winter months of long confinement it will contaminate the rest of the flock. Use a leg mite treatment followed by coating the legs with Vaseline to suffocate any remaining mite.

Worming

It is a good idea to worm birds before winter sets in. Use a powder wormer such as Flubenvet or Verm-X mixed in with the feed in accordance with the manufacturer's recommendations. Adding a little cod liver oil when mixing the powder into the feed will help it to stick evenly to the pellets, ensuring all the birds are treated and avoiding wasting lots of powder. Alternatively, use layers' pellets impregnated with a wormer.

A Poultry Manicure

It is very easy to overlook problems relating to the birds' legs, feet and beak. Perhaps it is understandable why these parts of the birds' bodies often appear a little neglected, but it is a neglect that can eventually lead to some very serious consequences. Regular checks must be made to make sure that these areas are not overgrown and causing problems for them. Regular cleaning and trimming will help to keep legs and feet clean and free from clogging, especially during the periods of bad, wet weather which are just around the corner.

Toenails

Overgrown toenails can become hard and twisted, making it difficult for the birds to both walk and perch. The nails on birds' feet grow very quickly, especially if they are on ground that does not give them the opportunity to wear down naturally. This can happen if the birds are confined to a run where the ground is soft or covered with grass; these surfaces don't provide any rough areas which might wear down the nails during the normal daily routine.

> *If birds are kept in a more natural, free-range environment with normal mixed ground cover, this will inevitably help to keep nail growth under control, but even in this situation nails will require regular checks.*

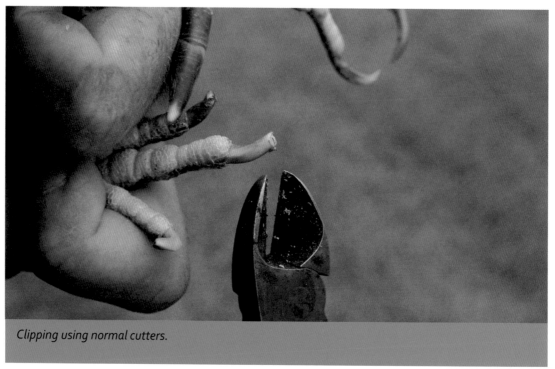

Clipping using normal cutters.

Trimming Nails

Hold the bird securely. If there is any likelihood of struggling, wrap it gently in a towel, but allow clear access to the feet. To trim the nails use a good, sharp pair of nail-clippers. Small wire-type cutters are also ideal. Do not use scissors as they are usually not strong enough to do the job. You can easily buy animal clippers made for this purpose, which are very easy and safe to use.

It may help to get someone to assist you by holding the bird while you are doing the trimming. Overgrown nails are certainly easy to see, and although there is no actual recommended length, they need to be cut back enough to enable the bird to walk in a normal manner. Really long nails curl and twist, and they can often be more awkward to cut back, as you may need to remove considerably more nail than normal just to get them straight. The length of nails will vary, as some breeds tend to have longer nails than others, but you can use your common sense and initiative to decide when they are too long.

Always take your time when trimming nails and carry out the task very carefully, removing only a small amount at a time. Take a close look and you will see that the end of the nail is paler in colour than the rear part of the nail; the paler part is what you are looking to remove. To do this, hold the foot securely and take away the ends of the nail, a small part at a time, making sure that you do not cut into the darker part at the rear of the nail. The lighter section has neither blood vessels nor nerves, and in principle is very similar to our own nails.

If you do go too far into the darker part of the nail it is liable to bleed, and although it may bleed quite heavily, it will soon stop, with the birds generally showing no signs of discomfort, so do not panic if this happens. Once you are satisfied that you have trimmed enough, gently file the sharp and square edges from the nail using an emery board or nail-file, and the bird will feel a lot better and will also be able to walk and perch more comfortably.

Cleaning Nails and Removing Dirt Balls

All chickens seem to love dirt and sludge. This is not a problem until they come into the coop and the mixture of dirt, shavings and droppings stick to their feet, which then become very soiled. This will eventually lead to the feet becoming so clogged with the mixture of damp dirt, bedding and droppings that large balls of dirt form on the toes and under the feet. The solid ball that becomes attached to the toenails can be very difficult to remove, but soaking the feet in water helps to remove it without damage, and prevents the birds losing a nail. If this ball is removed without first being softened it is very likely that the toenail will be removed together with the ball.

Remove the solid dirt balls by first soaking the feet in warm water until the lumps become soft. To do this, stand the bird in a bucket with a couple of inches of warm water and cover the bucket with a cloth. This will keep the bird calm while standing in the bucket. Alternatively, you could hold the feet under a running tap providing warm water until the dirt ball is soaked and softened.

You can also remove the balls dry by gently cutting into them, but doing this is more difficult and you can easily remove the nail together with the dirt. If you do decide to remove a dry dirt ball, make sure you proceed very slowly, and take great care to find exactly where the encrusted toes and nails are within the dirt ball prior to cutting.

Once the nails are both clean and trimmed it is a good idea to carefully file off any rough edges left by the trimming. Leaving rough edges creates a surface which will soon cause the nails to become clogged again with the same type of dirt ball that you have just removed.

Spurs

It is quite normal for birds, especially cockerels, to grow spurs, which appear from the rear of the leg. They can vary considerably in both length and appearance, but these spurs can actually give you

Hardened dirt balls on feet.

Scrubbing feet clean.

Cutting spurs.

a reasonably accurate idea of a bird's true age. They can grow quite long, and, in some cases, this can become such an issue that it can seriously affect a bird's mobility. I have seen a cock bird with spurs that had grown so long that they had curved upwards and were in fact growing back towards the bird's leg. If left unattended they would eventually have penetrated the leg, causing considerable suffering to the bird.

Removing Spurs the Old-fashioned Way

Removing spurs many years ago involved a method which used a hot, baked potato. You simply pushed it onto the spur and held it there for about ten minutes. The heat caused the spur to loosen, and it came away with no ill effects for the bird. Within just a few hours it would be feeling fit and well, and looking very relieved to be free of the large, awkward spur.

Old hens can also be found growing spurs, although these are much smaller than the ones that grow on cocks. There are still, however, occasions when they will need trimming. Carrying out these tasks can be classed as basic general maintenance, but it will help to keep the birds in good condition, and is necessary for their welfare and well-being.

Cut straight across the paler front part of the beak.

Trimming

Spurs can be very strong and quite difficult to trim as they are generally thick, solid and very hard, depending on the age of the bird. Trimming them is very similar to the way you trim both beaks and toenails, except for the thickness. You will need an exceptionally strong pair of cutters to remove the end of the spur, and as described earlier in the toenail section, only cut the end of the spur which is a lighter colour. When cutting spurs there is always a possibility that the pressure you use may cause the whole of the spur to come away. This is not a problem and does no harm to the bird, although it leaves behind a very sharp, pointed spur that has been growing underneath the original one. The result will be quite bloody, but this soon heals with no adverse effect on the bird, and it will soon grow again naturally.

Beak Clipping

The same principle applies to beaks, because they, too, can grow very quickly, causing birds discomfort, and in really bad cases it may prevent them from feeding. A regular check is always a very good idea to prevent any problems relating to excessively long beaks. To some extent, checks will depend on the breeds you keep, but it is a good idea to carry these out every three or four months, and to trim whenever it is required.

Again, trimming the beak works on the same principle as the toenails. Check the beak and look for the part that darkens. You just remove a small amount, and take only the pale part, as this will prevent any bleeding. When cutting the beak, do so straight across the paler front part, and then carefully and gently trim the square sides slightly to take the beak back towards its original point. Wrapping the bird in a towel will make holding it a lot easier, and will also help to give you more control over the bird, which helps to keep it calm and reduce stress. To finish, carefully file the edges, shaping the beak, and take great care, as it will bleed heavily if overtrimmed.

Commercial hybrids in intensive units are sometimes de-beaked to prevent cannibalism. This is a process that has been carried out for many years and is done by a qualified person with a tool specifically designed to carry out the task

Hold the wing open like a fan so you can clearly see the primary and secondary wing feathers.

Clipping the wing.

Wing clipped.

as humanely as possible. The beak is trimmed and automatically sealed by the machine. If this is not carried out in these large units, feather pecking and cannibalism will be a major problem. Although the practice may upset some people, it is actually carried out with the birds' welfare in mind.

Beaks sometimes get broken or cut off due to freak accidents, and missing beak portions will not grow back. Depending on how much of the beak is left, a bird may or may not be able to eat normally. If only a small amount is missing from one, or even both beak halves, the bird will probably be fine. However, if large portions of either the top or bottom section are gone, the bird will have difficulty in eating. The beak is used for picking up food and for cutting it, in the case of leaves, but is not required to either chew or crush food.

There are many chicken keepers who keep rescued hybrids, and often these birds will have a top beak that is shorter than the bottom beak. When you see these birds it can look quite strange, and gives them an unusual appearance. Although the practice prevents feather pecking, it in no way affects a bird's ability to both eat and drink.

Wing Clipping

There are times when you will need to clip your chickens' wings. This is mostly required when birds are free range and you need to keep them within your own area. If the birds can fly, it can create issues with neighbours, or they could meet a fox or an angry dog. It is not cruel and does not in any way hurt the bird. In fact, you only need to clip one wing in order to make the bird uncertain of its balance when looking to take off, but many people do clip both.

This is better done as a two-person job, with one person holding the bird while the other performs the trimming. Once you have caught the bird, give it a little time to calm down and relax, then spread out the wing to reveal the primary feathers. Hold the wing away from the body and select the feathers you are going to cut. The primary

Clean gently round the eye using a sterile cloth and medicated eye-wash.

Occassonally you will have to wash your bird.

feathers are generally longer than the others, and are in many cases lighter in colour. There are about ten of these, and they are the ones you need to cut. Use a sharp pair of scissors and clip about two-thirds of the feather, but do not forget that feathers do have a blood supply, so don't cut too far back.

When carrying out any of these procedures, and certainly if doing so for the first time, please refer to the photos which demonstrate how to do the job in a correct and safe manner. Also, do bear in mind that when you are trimming it is inevitable that you will occasionally go a little too far – I'm sure you've all done it when cutting your own fingernails! If it does happen, it is better to keep the bird separate from the flock until the bleeding stops. This does not take long and will prevent any problems from starting with the other birds.

Treating Chickens' Eyes

You will occasionally need to treat injuries to your birds. Eye and beak injuries are not uncommon, especially if a predator attacks. You can, in fact, even take care of a blind chicken, or learn how to

feed a bird with a broken beak.

Damage to a chicken's eyes can also occur during fights within the flock. A little pirate patch on a chicken would look rather silly (and would be awkward for the bird!), so cleaning the eye and keeping the bird isolated is about the best you can do. Clean the eyes with non-medicated eyewash intended for pets or for humans. A chicken will be fine if blind in one eye, but if it was blind in both, you would need to cage it if you decided to keep it.

Washing Birds' Feathers

Birds will keep their own feathers reasonably clean by using dust baths and by preening, but any birds that become exceptionally soiled (including around the vent) will need to be cleaned by the keeper. The best way of doing this is to wash them with a suitable product. Johnson's Baby Shampoo is a favourite with keepers, or you could use a standard pet type shampoo, or even one with an insect control/prevention additive.

When washing, always make sure the birds do not become too stressed. This is best achieved by

Alert eyes and a bright red comb – the perfect picture of health.

Certain vaccines come in two separate vials, one containing a powder, the other a liquid. Once mixed together you have just an hour to administer them. After that time they will be of no use. Find a suitable place to dispose of the leftovers.

Instructions for administering vaccines

Wear suitable outer clothing and footwear, preferably something that can be disinfected easily after use, especially when vaccinating for Newcastle disease, chicken pox or laryngotracheitis.

Thoroughly clean and disinfect all equipment used during the vaccinations.

Be sure of the disease you are vaccinating against, its correct diagnosis and the method to be used.

wrapping them in a towel, as this both helps to keep the bird under control and gives a sense of safety and security. Most birds are actually quite easy to handle and will usually stand in a bowl of warm water. Soak the plumage thoroughly, rub in the shampoo and then rinse – not unlike washing your own hair, in many respects. If the weather is warm the birds can be left to dry naturally, but a hairdryer will be required during colder periods to make sure the birds do not become chilled.

Treating Your Birds

Most, if not all of the ailments detailed in the A-Z of Ailments section can be treated with appropriate medication, and the following section is included to explain the process and put it in a practical context regarding a number of the ailments listed.

Vaccines and Medicines

Vaccines come in bottles containing doses sufficient for 500 or 1000 birds, but even if you need only a small quantity they still work out very economically, and any unused vaccine can be destroyed responsibly. The contents can be administered through injection, special applicator, eye drops or mixed with water.

There are two types of vaccine used on poultry; 'dead' vaccines and 'live' vaccines.

Dead Vaccines

These are produced from the cultures of disease organisms that have been treated by laboratories to make them harmless. Although dead they can still be used to create immunity, but it usually takes two doses to stimulate that immunity.

Live Vaccines

These are divided into two types; one contains an organism close to the one that causes the disease, but that does *not* cause the birds to show clinical symptoms. These are grown in the laboratory and, due to being related to the original organism, will stimulate the immune system. In the other type the organism is modified to provide increased immunity *without* actually producing the disease.

Live vaccines can produce birds with no visible signs of disease, but they could be carriers that can affect other non-vaccinated birds in the flock.

How to Give Injections

There are several methods of giving injections, the most common being in the breast or the thigh. If you have no previous experience of giving injections then go to a qualified person who will either administer the vaccine or show you how to carry out the task correctly. In all circumstances, before giving any injections do make sure that *all* the air bubbles are removed from the syringe.

Vaccinating against:

Marek's disease

The injections need to be given on day 1, or hatch day.

The vaccine is given by injection under the skin behind the neck.

Keep a check on the chickens for the next 12 weeks.

Fowl cholera

Only vaccinate after the disease has been correctly diagnosed.

Administer in water using a live attenuated oral vaccine.

Give two injections of oil-emulsion bacterins 4 weeks apart

Infectious bronchitis

This disease requires a live bronchitis vaccine.

Combine this with the Newcastle vaccine and carry out the process at between 10 and 35 days old.

Inject a dead virus vaccine into the muscle or under the skin between the ages of 14 and 18 weeks

Fowl pox

Vaccinate when and if the problem exists by using the 'web stick' method.

Vaccinate by dipping the slotted needles of the applicator into the vaccine, then push through the wing web.

Do it from 1 day old and up to 2 weeks for chicks and repeat the treatment when the chicks reach 8 weeks of age.

Laryngotracheitis

Vaccinate using a live vaccine.

Vaccinate only if the disease exists and has been correctly diagnosed.

Given by eye drop at 4 weeks or older

Fowl cholera

Only vaccinate after the disease has been correctly diagnosed.

Administer in water using a live attenuated oral vaccine.

Give two injections of oil-emulsion bacterins 4 weeks apart.

Newcastle disease

Treat using either nose or eye drops or through the drinking water. Administer to one-day-old chicks.

Administer the dead virus by injecting under the skin or into the muscle to young birds before egg production.

Use a combined Newcastle/Infectious bronchitis vaccine through drinking water or drops to chicks between 10 and 35 days old.

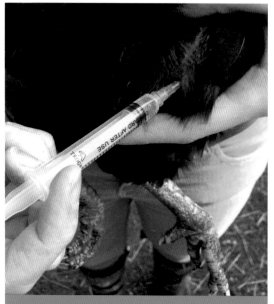

Do not attempt to administer an injection unless you have been trained.

Fallen Stock

For the commercial poultry keeper fallen stock, which includes birds which have died of natural causes or disease together with any others which have died for reasons other than human consumption, must be dealt with appropriately. The National Fallen Stock Company is available to help with disposal and advises on disease prevention as part of the National Fallen Stock Scheme.

Of course illness is always a possibility when looking after animals, and inevitably the backyard chicken keeper too will eventually experience losses. Whilst being exempt from the rules covering 'fallen stock', if you do suspect that a bird has died of a 'notifiable disease', you must tell your local Animal Health Office immediately. Currently, in the case of chickens the only notifiable diseases are Newcastle disease and avian influenza, both thankfully very rare.

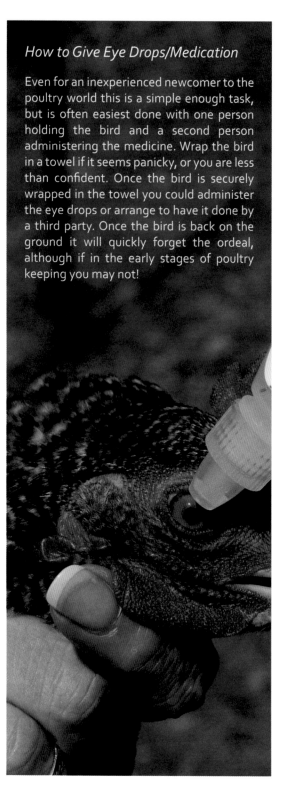

How to Give Eye Drops/Medication

Even for an inexperienced newcomer to the poultry world this is a simple enough task, but is often easiest done with one person holding the bird and a second person administering the medicine. Wrap the bird in a towel if it seems panicky, or you are less than confident. Once the bird is securely wrapped in the towel you could administer the eye drops or arrange to have it done by a third party. Once the bird is back on the ground it will quickly forget the ordeal, although if in the early stages of poultry keeping you may not!

Transporting Poultry

When transporting poultry for economic or commercial purposes you should:

- plan your journeys thoroughly and keep the duration to a minimum.

- ensure the birds are fit to travel and check them regularly.

- ensure vehicle loading and unloading facilities are constructed and maintained to avoid injury and suffering.

- ensure those handling the birds are competent and don't use violence or any methods likely to cause fear, injury or suffering.

- provide sufficient floor space and height allowance.

- provide water, feed and rest as needed.

These are, however, also excellent guidelines for the garden or backyard chicken keeper to bear in mind when transporting just a few birds, perhaps for the purposes of showing them.

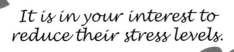

It is in your interest to reduce their stress levels.

Documentation

At present this is only required if you transport your poultry for commercial purposes. Any journeys over sixty five kilometres (about forty miles) will require a valid transport certificate known as a transporter authorisation, with different rules for journeys below eight hours (type 1 transporter authorisation) and for those above eight hours (type 2 transporter authorisation). For most chicken keepers common sense and an adherence to the above six points will ensure good practice.

If you are intending to show, a purpose-made carrier will be a worthwhile investment.

Carry Boxes

For the small-scale chicken keeper looking to transport just a couple of birds, safety is best achieved with a carry box. There are an infinite number of options available, from a basic flat pack cardboard box to hi-spec designer options. If you are thinking of investing in a carry box, the price of buying a ready-made one will vary considerably, depending on the type, size and style you require. There are some excellent ready-made boxes to choose from, but you could also have one of your own designs made up for you, but the problem will probably be the cost – custom-made boxes tend to be expensive.

Whatever you decide, whether going for a top of the range model or making one yourself, make sure the box comes up to the standard you require. Consider the following suggestions before purchasing your box:

- Will it have good ventilation?

- Will there be space enough for the number of birds being moved? True bantams are very small and a box will normally house several. Standard bantams (with large fowl equivalents) are a little larger, but large fowl will normally travel at no more than two to a box.

- Comfort (is there room for movement inside and for the birds to stand, but with suitable restrictions to prevent injury whilst being transported)?

- Is the box designed to prevent excessive build up of heat? Excessive heat during transporting could kill birds.

- Is the floor of the box made using an anti-slip material? Both astro-turf (my own personal favourite) or rubber will be ideal and can be easily cleaned. Carpet is an alternative but will need to be disposed of after a couple of trips as it becomes soiled. For taking birds to shows a layer of saw dust will help stop them becoming soiled.

Culling birds is an occasional necessity and must only ever be done by a trained person .

Cleaning the Box

Always clean a box or carry case after each journey. It is common sense, but also creates a safeguard if you are ever checked at any time when transporting the birds, and will ensure that the *next* bird carried is not infected by its predecessor. Today biosecurity is a necessary preventative measure. If we all do as required, then we shall be able to carry on with our poultry as normal and, hopefully, with no future problems.

Culling/Dispatching Birds

The subject of culling poultry is a very difficult one to approach; these days many people tend to view it as cruel and find the practice unacceptable. There are, however, two distinct poultry sectors today. One is the traditional industry sector with a very pragmatic view of the value of their birds, and the other is the more recent garden or backyard sector, which could be termed as hobby or leisure. The latter keepers, at least in part, grew out of a reaction to the cruelties of the battery sector and the setting up of the British Hen Welfare Trust (or Battery Hen Welfare Trust, as it was originally

called). This sector views the keeping of a few hens as not dissimilar to keeping a cat or a dog as a family pet, but combines elements of downshifting into the equation together with growing your own veg and a degree of self-sufficiency. Although there is a grey area between the two, with an increasing number of compassionate commercial concerns and some more traditional backyard keepers who still view the birds as 'earning their keep' by producing eggs. Garden and backyard keepers are more likely to call in a vet, and a whole new sector has recently evolved to provide this service.

Whether or not you choose to call in a vet, culling is an occasional necessity when keeping poultry, whether you do it for food or just for pleasure – too many cockerels, for example, will create problems, therefore, like it or not, there is always a time when this has to be carried out. There are a number of traditional and accepted reasons for culling, the main one being faults or defects in birds – deformities need to be culled out to both keep breeds in top quality condition and also to stop the unnecessary suffering of any seriously deformed birds. It is a well-established fact that if these birds are grown on they rarely seem to get any better, and in many cases suffer from numerous problems

Welsummer cockerel.

Culling using a hand-held dispatcher.

until they eventually die; allowing suffering is cruel and should be avoided.

As regards the problem of breeding an excess of cocks, I think most countries suffer from the inevitable neighbour complaints about them crowing. Such complaints have caused some very serious disputes which we really need to avoid if the enjoyment of and increase in backyard poultry keeping is to continue. You nearly always seem to hatch more cocks than hens and they are almost impossible to re-home. This inevitably leaves a number of male birds that are not needed and costly to keep, although this obviously does not apply if the birds are being grown on for the table, and this too is now becoming ever more popular as we all want to rear our own fresh food; there is a great empowerment to knowing where that food came from and also how it was reared. When you have tasted fresh corn reared chicken you quickly realise there is a huge difference from standard supermarket chicken.

To cull most poultry is not a difficult task and has traditionally been done by dislocating the neck just below the base of the head – this can be done either by hand or by using a hand held dispatcher or a wall mounted dispatcher. The latter two implements will make the job a lot simpler to perform and, if used correctly, should prevent unnecessary suffering for the birds at the hands of an inexperienced keeper.

Dislocation needs to be both quick and positive, and to do this with certainty and confidence (a lack of which are the main causes of unnecessary suffering) takes practice. It is something best described and taught by an experienced poultry keeper with many years' experience of performing this action. There is never any excuse for causing unnecessary suffering to birds, but there is also the added problem that some of the larger breeds require a considerable amount of strength to cull them both quickly and cleanly.

Chickens for the Table

Chickens reared for meat are commonly known as broilers. Commercially the birds are reared intensively in large units run at a constant temperature with fully automatic water and feeding systems. The object is to grow the birds to a saleable weight as quickly as possible – their normal life span is around 6 to 8 weeks. Culling on this scale is done on a production line basis, mostly by electrocution, but if you are a keeper with just a few birds it will most likely be done manually.

Hand Culling

Hand culling has been carried out for many hundreds of years. The bird is held securely in one hand, with the other hand around the neck. Place two fingers below the head, tilt it slightly back and pull sharply whilst keeping the head tilted back. This dislocates the neck and the bird is dead almost instantly. It will continue to move as the nerves will still operate for a short time after it is dead; do not be surprised by this movement as it is a natural reaction. To carry out this procedure both quickly and cleanly needs practice. You *will* need advice and guidance to carry this out yourself, but once you have mastered the act it is relatively simple to perform, though somewhat unpleasant.

The Hand-held Dispatcher

This method is a lot easier than doing it by hand. It is, however, really only suitable for smaller birds and can, if it is not carried out carefully, become a little messy. The dispatcher is similar in size and appearance to a set of pliers and if used incorrectly it can cut into the neck and, in extreme cases, remove the head from the body. The equipment is used in a similar way to your fingers, with the dispatcher going *across* the neck in the same place, just below the base of the head. You tighten the clamp onto the neck, press hard and twist – this action dislocates the neck and the job is completed. They are unsuitable for larger breeds of poultry as they are not strong enough and, in my own opinion, make culling even more unpleasant and awkward to carry out.

The Wall-mounted Dispatcher

Without doubt the easiest and the quickest method, it is both easy to use and control, even

for an inexperienced poultry keeper. They can, however, be quite expensive, but they are very effective and easy to operate. The dispatcher fits onto a wall and has a lever that you pull down onto the bird's neck; with this action all you need to do is give a very gentle pull to ensure the neck has been properly dislocated – there is rarely any mess and it is instant. There are adjustments on the unit handle so it can be set for different sizes of bird, but we have set ours on one setting and it works very well with no problems. Using one of these dispatchers has the added advantage of you having both hands free; this is helpful if you are a beginner and makes the task much simpler.

There are other methods of dispatching, including bullets (particularly unsafe, in my opinion) electrical stunning with neck cutting and electrical killing, but if you are a small-scale or backyard keeper it is most likely you will use one of the neck dislocation methods if you decide to cull. If your interests are commercial then you will already be aware of the available alternatives.

Culling Chicks

This is one of the hardest and most unpleasant tasks for a chicken keeper. You will, however, always get chicks which are weak or poor quality, cannot walk, perhaps with severely twisted toes or many other different faults. There is no excuse for rearing these birds as they will never enjoy a decent quality of life, and there are methods suitable for use with birds of this age, including small hand-held dispatchers. Some traditional methods used in the past would be viewed as brutal today, but culling will always be with us, and on occasion it is a question of welfare to decide to cull – the only question remaining is whether you or someone else will do it.

When culling becomes inevitable, allow the birds to settle and not become stressed. Catch them when it is dusk or dark as they are then at their most relaxed. Also, be certain that you are capable of carrying out the cull in an efficient and humane manner.

The Legal Position

In the same way that the law seeks to protect a bird's welfare *during* its life, it also sets out to protect a bird's welfare during slaughter. The weight of the legislation deals with the commercial industry, emphasising that a bird *must* be rendered unconscious prior to slaughter. Given the numbers killed each day it is only correct that this sector is the main target for legislation. If you do decide to cull your own birds then the two easiest available legal methods to smallholders and other small-scale keepers are neck dislocation and decapitation. Decapitation is frowned upon by the Humane Slaughter Association as birds can show continued brain activity for thirty seconds after the cut is made. They also express concern about neck dislocation as they do not regard it as instantaneous. Their recommended methods require electrical or mechanical concussion stunning, resulting in instantaneous insensibility. This must be followed up immediately by a method of killing – usually bleeding or neck dislocation – whilst the bird is still unconscious. The equipment required for such stunning is very costly, and using it commercially requires a license.

The official position is that the welfare of animals at the time of slaughter or killing is covered by European Union Directive 93/119 and UK regulations. These rules state that animals must never be submitted to any avoidable stress, pain or suffering, and if slaughtered for commercial purposes, must be handled, stunned and killed using specific methods by licensed slaughtermen. There are also special arrangements when specific slaughter methods are used for religious purposes such as the Halal or Kosher killing of chickens. Religious slaughter can only take place in an approved slaughterhouse. These welfare requirements also apply to on-farm slaughter of birds, although an owner killing an animal for private consumption does not need a slaughter licence, and this is how the law applies to today's typical UK chicken keeper. There are, however, proposals from Europe to change the law, but these changes are always under discussion, so it is always wise to keep an eye on relevant websites. These changes will most likely apply only to commercial operations but try to keep abreast of any new legislation affecting you – ignorance of the law has never been accepted as an excuse!

Finally I leave you with 6 points to remember:

- Chickens need daily care and attention; if you cannot supply this you will need someone who can look after the birds on a permanent basis or in your absence.

- They always need a constant supply of clean water and dry food.

- Their housing has to be secure and predator proof.

- If you want a supply of eggs but do not intend to breed, a cockerel is not required.

- Housing should be moved regularly to keep ground clean, fresh and free from parasites which could harm your birds.

- The Welfare Code of Practice and several other regulations cover the keeping of chickens. These must be adhered to.

Happy, healthy hen keeping!

RESOURCES

General Suppliers

Ascott Smallholding Supplies
Units 21/22, Whitewalls, Easton Grey
Malmesbury, SN16 0RD
www.ascot.biz | Tel: 0845 130 6285

The Domestic Fowl Trust
Station Road, Honeybourne, Evesham, WR11 7QZ
www.domesticfowltrust.co.uk | Tel: 01386 833083

Poultry Feed

Allen & Page
Norfolk Mill, Shipdham, Thetford, IP25 7SD
www.allenandpage.com | Tel: 01362 822900

Marriage's Feeds
Chelmer Mills, New Street, Chelmsford, CM1 1PN.
www.marriagefeeds.co.uk | Tel: 01245 354455

Fancy Feed Company
Four Elms Mills, Bardfield Saling, Braintree,
Essex , CM7 5EJ
www.fancyfeedcompany.co.uk | Tel: 01371 850247

Hetty's Hen House (Hentastic Range)
Unit L, Tribune Drive, Trinity Trading Estate,
Sittingbourne, ME10 2PG
www.hettyshenhouse.com | Tel: 01795 472 096

Hygiene & Medicines

Verm-X
Huish Champflower, Somerset, TA4 2HQ
www.verm-x.com | Tel: 0870 850 2313

Barrier Animal Healthcare
36 Haverscroft Industrial Estate, New Road,
Attleborough, Norfolk, NR17 1YE
www.redmite.com | Tel: 01953 456363

Eradibait
Ilex EnviroSciences Limited, North Hangar,
Wickenby Airfield, Lincoln, LN3 5AX
www.eradi-products.com | Tel: 01673 885175

Biolink Ltd.
Halifax Way, Pocklington,
York, YO42 1NR
www.biolinklimited.co.uk | Tel: 01759 303158

Housing

Brinsea
Station Road, Sandford, Somerset, BS25 5RA
www.brinsea.co.uk | Tel: 0845 226 0120

Flyte so Fancy
The Cottage, Pulham, Dorchester, DT2 7DX
www.flytesofancy.co.uk | Tel: 01300 345229

Green Frog Designs
The Empire Farm, Throop Road, Templecombe,
Somerset, BA8 0HR
www.greenfrogdesigns.co.uk | Tel: 01963 37563

Osprey Limited
Stokewood Road, Long Lane Industrial Estate
Craven Arms, Shropshire, SY7 8NR
www.bec.co.uk | Tel: 01588 673821

Feeders & Drinkers

Osprey Limited
Stokewood Road, Long Lane Industrial Estate
Craven Arms, Shropshire, SY7 8NR
www.bec.co.uk | Tel: 01588 673821

Grandpa's Feeders
126 Clevelode, Guarlford, Malvern, WR13 6PA
www.grandpasfeeders.co.uk | Tel: 01684 311 729

Incubators

Brinsea
Station Road, Sandford, Somerset, BS25 5RA
www.brinsea.co.uk | Tel: 0845 226 0120

Fencing

Electric Fencing Direct
Traprain Cottage, 7 Traprain, Haddington,
EH41 4PY
www.electricfencing.co.uk | Tel: 01360 440611

Useful Websites

www.chickenvet.com
Providing owners of pet chickens, fancy fowl and
small flock keepers' advice on the care, health and
well-being of their birds.

www.facebook.co.uk/poultrytalk.com
Very useful advice provided by a friendly team of
experienced and knowledgeable poultry keepers.

www. poultrykeeper.com
Over 550 articles and many useful resources for
the hobbyist interested in keeping chickens,
ducks, geese and other poultry.

www.bbschoice.co.uk | Tel: 01280 738606
BB'S Choice is a selection of only the best tried and
tested products recommended by the author.